THE AMERICAN SUPREME COURT

The American

THE CHICAGO HISTORY OF AMERICAN CIVILIZATION
Daniel J. Boorstin, EDITOR

Supreme Court

By Robert G. McCloskey

 THE UNIVERSITY OF CHICAGO PRESS
CHICAGO AND LONDON

TO MY WIFE

THE UNIVERSITY OF CHICAGO PRESS, CHICAGO 60637

The University of Chicago Press, Ltd., London

ISBN: 0–226–55673–5 (clothbound); 0–226–55675–1 (paperbound)
Library of Congress Catalog Card Number: 60–14235

89 88 87 86 85 84 83 82   15 16 17 18 19 20

Editor's Preface

Today the strength of the Supreme Court of the United States seems the best proof that our political system is capable of firmness and dignity. Yet President Washington had difficulty finding men of national stature willing to sit on so inconsequential a court. Historians still disagree over what powers the Founding Fathers intended to give these judges. Certainly the Founding Fathers had no blueprint for such a court. Many of them would be astonished and most might be shocked that any branch of the central government had attained such power. Of all the achievements of American civilization none is more the accidental by-product of our past.

The history of the Supreme Court, and especially the story of judicial review to which this volume is mainly devoted, is the surprising account of how a few men have used powers of dubious legality to uphold the rule of law in American life. There is no more ironic aspect of our history.

Every generation, while finding its own uses for the Court, has preserved the Court as a symbol of the need for limits and for continuity in a nation of novelties. The Supreme Court has

thus become the American political conscience, a kind of sec-
ular papacy, a new search in every generation for what the
more large-minded and more foresighted of the Founders might
have meant if they were alive. It is the Great Remembrancer
of our foundations.

Actually the Court has become a monument both to our need
to search for historical consistency and to the limits of such
consistency. Through the history of the Court we see that men
can serve a traditional purpose only by changing instruments
and by shifting ground. And we discover how great judges
make the cautionary wisdom of the past speak in the technical
language of the common law.

In the present volume, Mr. McCloskey gives us a concise and
dramatic account of that part of the Court's work which has
been closest to the mainstream of American politics. All the
crises in our political history have sooner or later been stated
in legal terms. Mr. McCloskey shows us how the major changes
in our political and economic life have been moderated and
justified by the Supreme Court.

The importance of the Supreme Court has come not only
from the Court's insistence on measuring the present against
the past, "needs" against "rights," opinion against law, but also
from the desire of the American people to take the Court's
decisions seriously. From time to time it has been said that the
Court—by its decisions about slavery, about the New Deal, or
about educational equality—has made trouble for the nation.
It would be more accurate to say that the American people
have made trouble for themselves by listening reverently and
obediently to men who remind them of their past, who prefer
legality to popularity. The uncanny American reverence for

Editor's Preface

law has made possible the uncanny power and dignity of the American Supreme Court.

By relating the history of the Supreme Court to other aspects of American civilization, Mr. McCloskey serves the purposes of the "Chicago History of American Civilization." This series aims to make each aspect of our culture a window to all our history. The series contains two kinds of books: a *chronological* group, which provides a coherent narrative of American history from its beginning to the present day; and a *topical* group, which deals with the history of varied and significant aspects of American life. This book is one of the topical group. Sixteen titles in the series have now been published, and twenty-odd are in preparation.

DANIEL J. BOORSTIN

Author's Preface

This book deals with the work of the Supreme Court of the United States as a constitutional tribunal, exercising the power of judicial review. It does not purport to describe the activity of the Court as a whole; much less is it a history of constitutional law in the widest possible sense, treating of constitutional developments that have been brought about by legislative and executive action, or by the more subtle process we call custom. Finally, because it is a brief book, I cannot of course even claim that it covers the story of judicial review comprehensively. The chapters are interpretive essays in the history of judicial review. They deal with aspects of that history that seem to me important and interesting, but they omit material that might legitimately seem equally important or interesting to another.

My aim has been, within this compass, to understand the way the Supreme Court has conducted itself to achieve its results, the role it has played in American life. I have been most concerned, as the text will reveal, to see the Court as an agency in the American governing process, an agency with a mind and a will and an influence of its own. Greatly as we may respect

John Marshall, not many sophisticated persons would now take these words of his very seriously: "Judicial power, as contradistinguished from the power of the laws, has no existence. Courts are the mere instruments of the law, and can will nothing."

Yet there has been too little effort, I believe, to project a contrary view back into judicial history in order to see what the Court *was*, if it was not what Marshall asserted. And because this has not been done, as I am at pains to suggest in the epilogue to this volume, we are not prepared as we should be to evaluate the Court of today, either as critics or as defenders.

Table of Contents

THE AMERICAN SUPREME COURT

I

The Genesis and Nature of
Judicial Power

On June 21, 1788, when the convention of New Hampshire voted 57 to 46 to approve the proposed national constitution, the requirement of nine ratifying states was fulfilled and the United States of America sprang into legal being. Opportunity for instant creation of this magnitude occurs only in fiction and law, and the delegates did not underrate their historic moment. They were careful to specify that it came at one o'clock in the afternoon, for they feared that Virginia might act that very evening and claim a share in the honor. They need not have worried. The Virginians were in for three more days of oratory, mostly by Patrick Henry, before their state's proud name could be added to the list.

Fifteen months later, President Washington accomplished another of these portentous juridical feats by signing the Judiciary Act of 1789, which was to be called many years afterward "probably the most important and the most satisfactory Act ever passed by Congress." The latter-day eulogist was himself a Supreme Court justice, and his good opinion of a law that made him one of the most august figures in the nation is not surprising; a long roll of eminent statesmen since 1789 could be called to testify on the other side. But hardly one of them would dispute his opinion that the Act was extremely important, for it not only established the far-flung system of federal courts but boldly defined their jurisdiction, and especially that of the Supreme Court, in such a way that the states, Congress, and the President could be held subject to judicial authority.

Finally, on February 2, 1790, some of the men who had received these high commissions and whose duty it therefore was to give living force to these paper enactments, assembled in the Royal Exchange building in New York and organized as the Supreme Court of the United States. The occasion was solemn, and the newspapers followed it closely, passing on to the people every crumb of detail about this third great department of their young national republic. Yet neither the press nor the people nor the justices themselves could quite know how momentous the day was, and there is good evidence that they did not. Only four of the six men Washington had chosen to adorn the Supreme Court turned up for that first official meeting. Robert H. Harrison declined appointment, apparently because he thought his judicial post as chancellor of Maryland was more important; and John Rutledge, though officially a member of the Court in its first three terms, never attended a session and soon resigned to accept the chief justiceship of South Carolina. Looking back, we can see that the first meeting of the Supreme Court of the United States was one of the mileposts in the history of jurisprudence. We can see that the ratifying of the Constitution and the signing of the Judiciary Act had, when taken together, opened great wells of judicial power, and that the four justices who sat together in the Royal Exchange that winter were inaugurating a governmental enterprise of vast and unprecedented dimensions. But the principals were looking forward, not back, and the future must have seemed cloudy.

In the nature of the case they would not have known much about the prospects of their Court and the Constitution, for the very good reason that so little about either had been firmly decided. The delegates who framed the Constitution have been traditionally and deservedly praised for producing a document that could earn the approval of such diverse states as Massachusetts and Georgia and such diverse men as John Adams and Thomas Jefferson (neither of whom, by the way, attended the Federal Convention). But this congenial result had been achieved not only by compromise but by forbearance. The Constitution clearly established a few principles about which there was no serious colonial disagreement, for example, the representative system for choosing officials and the separation of powers between the departments of the national government. It compromised a few more troublesome issues like the question of equal state representation versus representation based on population, and the question of the slave trade. But still weightier difficulties that might have prevented ratification were either left severely alone by the Founding Fathers or treated in ambiguous clauses that passed the problems on to posterity.

No one quite knew, for example, what was meant when the Constitution endowed Congress with power "to regulate commerce among foreign nations, and among the several states";

or to make all laws "necessary and proper" for carrying out the national government's other powers; or when it was asserted that the Constitution as well as laws and treaties made by the nation were "the supreme law of the land." No one was sure how the "ex post facto" clause or the "contract clause" would restrict state inroads on the rights of property-holders. Some had hopes and others had suspicions about the meaning of these and other enigmatic phrases in the document. But if either the hopes or the suspicions had been fully warranted by clear language in the Constitution itself, it seems most unlikely that ratification would have been possible. The issue underlying these uncertainties was no less than this: whether a nation or a league of sovereign states was created by the Constitution. That was the question still awaiting decision in 1790, and until America began answering it, the full significance of New Hampshire's historic vote was a matter for guess work. If a true nation emerged as the future unfolded, then New Hampshire's action was unforgettable. If not, ratification would be seen as a comparatively minor incident in modern world history.

As for the Supreme Court, its future was even more uncertain. The Constitution has comparatively little to say about the Court or the federal judiciary in general. The "judicial power of the United States," whatever it may be, is vested in the Supreme Court and in such other courts as Congress may establish. But the composition of the Court, including the number of its members, is left for congressional decision; and, while federal judges cannot be removed except by impeachment, there is nothing to prevent Congress from creating additional judgeships whenever it chooses. Furthermore, although the judicial power "extends" to a variety of cases described in Article III, section 2, the second paragraph of that section significantly qualifies what the first seems to have granted, and gives Congress power to control the Supreme Court's jurisdiction over appeals from lower courts. Since the cases that reach the Court directly without first being heard in other courts are comparatively minor in quantity or importance, this legislative authority over appeals (over the "appellate jurisdiction") is a license for Congress to decide whether the Supreme Court will be a significant or a peripheral factor in American government.

Most important of all, the Constitution makes no explicit statement about the nature of the Court's power even when a case admittedly falls within its jurisdiction. Some of the uncertainties outlined above were resolved, temporarily at any rate, by the passage of the Judiciary Act. Its famous Section 25 gave the Supreme Court power to reverse or affirm state court decisions which had denied claims based on the federal Constitution, treaties, or laws. This meant that such cases could be reached by the Supreme Court through its appellate jurisdiction. But suppose a state court had denied such a claim under the federal Constitution and the Supreme Court of the United States reversed on the ground that the state court's interpretation of the Constitution was in error. And suppose further that the state court obstinately continued to insist upon its own interpretation. Was there anything in the Constitution to guarantee that the Supreme Court's opinion would prevail, that the Supreme Court's authority was superior to state courts? Or suppose, to carry the matter a step further, that the state court had held a federal law invalid as conflicting with the *national* Constitution and the Supreme Court *agreed* with this holding, thus asserting its authority to overthrow an act of Congress. Does the Constitution make it *clear* that the Court has this final authority of "judicial review" over national legislative enactments?

The answer to both questions is a fairly solid "no." As for state decisions it has been argued that the "supreme law of the land" clause and the clause extending the judicial power to cases arising under the Constitution do make it clear that the Supreme Court was intended to be pre-eminent on questions of constitutional interpretation. If the Constitution is supreme and the Supreme Court has jurisdiction over cases involving the Constitution, then it follows that the Court's word on such matters is paramount over all others—so the argument runs. But in the first place this reasoning is not unassailable, for as defenders of states' rights were later passionately to insist, the fact that the Constitution is supreme does not settle the question of who decides what the Constitution means. And in the second place enthusiasts for judicial review have never quite been able to explain why so formidable a power was granted by implication rather than by flat statement. As for judicial review of congressional acts, the support in the language of the Constitution was even more suppositious, and arguments for the authority derived solely from that language seem inevitably to beg the question.

None of this is to say that the framers of the Constitution would have been surprised to see the Supreme Court exercising the power of judicial review in some form, both as against the states and as against Congress. Indeed there is ample evidence that most of them who had thought about it expected that the Court would do so, however distressing it is that they failed to make their expectations explicit. But neither the framers nor the ratifying state conventions (whose views are in some ways more relevant to the issue) had any general understanding about the particular form that the judicial review would take and the role that the Supreme Court would therefore assume.

The Genesis and Nature of Judicial Power

Some, like Alexander Hamilton, certainly hoped that the justices would act as general monitors, broadly supervising the other branches of government and holding them to the path of constitutional duty, though even he seems to have conceived this exalted notion only after the Convention's adjournment. Others, like Robert Yates, also of New York, feared that the Court would so regard its function. But James Madison, the highest possible authority on the Constitution's intent, though apparently expecting the Supreme Court to disallow laws that *clearly* contravened the Constitution, by no means conceded that the Court could apply its negative judgment to more debatable points or that the judicial pronouncements were intended to be final and binding on the other branches of government. And the evidence of both the Convention and the ratification controversy suggests that other participants were equally doubtful about these questions and that many more had simply not considered the matter at all.

In short, neither the words of the Constitution nor the provable intent of those who framed and ratified it justified in 1790 any certitude about the scope or finality of the Court's power to superintend either the states or Congress. The most that can be said is that language and intent did not *preclude* the Court from becoming the puissant tribunal of later history.

GREAT EXPECTATIONS

Nevertheless those four men in the Royal Exchange, though without any ironclad assurances, might well have had a strong hunch that destiny sat beside them, that the Constitution would be transfigured from a bitterly debated paper enactment into a venerated symbol of Americanism, and that the Court would emerge as the chief expounder of its mysteries and a beneficiary of its prestige. They must have realized that by tradition and temperament the new nation was ripe for such developments.

For the Constitution was potentially the convergence point for all the ideas about fundamental law that had been current in America since the colonization period. Of course the notion of a law-above-government, a "higher" law, was well known throughout the Western world, but the colonists had given it a special domestic cast, infusing it with interpretations drawn from their own unique experience. While most Europeans thought of higher law as exercising a moral restraint on government, they did not argue that this moral limit was legally enforceable, that it was positive law, practically binding the governors. Even before the Revolutionary controversy, Americans had found it easy to assume that it was just that, for their own legislatures had long been literally bound by "higher law" in such forms as the colonial charters and decisions of the British Privy Council. But the struggle with England turned assumption into fiery conviction as the colonists argued that Parliament was forbidden, not only morally but literally, to transgress the rights Americans claimed under their charters and under the British Constitution. And after the break with England this now very American idea of a written, tangible higher law was further embodied in the new state constitutions and in the Articles of Confederation. The document of 1789 then could draw on this enormous fund of prestige that the higher-law idea had assimilated in America.

Such circumstances might help explain, at least initially, why the Constitution won such ready devotion. But the question remains, it might be said, why the Court should be chosen to share in and perpetuate the Constitution's glory. We have seen that the language of the Constitution is inconclusive on this matter and that the intentions of the framers were ambiguous. Jefferson, Madison and many other almost equally illustrious statesmen were later to argue that the Congress, the President, and even the individual states were, no less than the courts, guardians of the Constitution and coequal interpreters of its meaning. What warrant then had our four new judges for hoping that history would reject these rival claimants and confirm the Supreme Court's constitutional prerogative? To put the question somewhat differently, what made it likely, though perhaps not certain, that the Court would play the great part it has played in American life?

THE HIGHER-LAW BACKGROUND AND POPULAR SOVEREIGNTY

With the benefit of hindsight, it is not hard to find a number of answers to these questions. The common law traditions deriving from the great seventeenth-century English jurist, Sir Edward Coke, exalted judges above other folk, and that tradition was cherished by Americans with peculiar tenacity. The Federalists, who enjoyed political ascendancy during the first decade of the Republic's history, tried to use their temporary prestige to implant in the popular mind a respect for judges, so that Federalism might find a haven against the adversity of a Jeffersonian political victory. The very fact that the concept of judicial review was, at the outset, imperfectly understood was a point in its favor, for it enabled judges to build up the Court's power gradually and almost imperceptibly and its opponents thus found themselves in the frustrating position of those who fight shadows. These factors, among others, are surely relevant to the problem. But they are not sufficient to explain the Court's impending future; they seem to rest on a broader, underlying causal condition whose roots drive deeper into the subsoil of American political life.

To understand that condition it is necessary to look again at the climate of political opinion in eighteenth-century America and particularly at the quarter-century that preceded the Constitution. We have seen that the old doctrine of fundamental law was stimulated by the events and idea currents of the Revolutionary era. Now it must be observed that the movement for revolution also supplied a vital impetus for another, and in some ways, contradictory, notion—the theory of popular sovereignty. American pamphleteers had insisted on the principle of home rule; the Declaration of Independence had founded just government on the "consent of the governed"; the next and natural step was to regard the people as not only a consenting but a willing entity and to declare, as Jefferson later said, that "the will of the majority is in all cases to prevail." These reasonable and perhaps inevitable deductions from the Spirit of '76 were widely prevalent in America during the Articles of Confederation period. Many of the solid citizens deplored such "mad democracy" and longed to curb it, but they could not evade the fact that the will-of-the-people concept was now firmly planted in American minds as one of the premises of political thinking.

Yet plainly that concept conflicted with the doctrine of fundamental law which was also, and concurrently, treasured by Americans. Popular sovereignty suggests *will*; fundamental law suggests *limit*. The one idea conjures up the vision of an active, positive state; the other idea emphasizes the negative, restrictive side of the political problem. It may be possible to harmonize these seeming opposites by logical sleight of hand, by arguing that the doctrines of popular sovereignty and fundamental law were fused in the Constitution, which was a popularly willed limitation. But it seems unlikely that Americans in general achieved such a synthesis and far more probable, considering our later political history, that most of them retained the two ideas side by side. This propensity to hold contradictory ideas simultaneously is one of the most significant qualities of the American political mind at all stages of national history, and it helps substantially in explaining the rise to power of the United States Supreme Court.

For with their political hearts thus divided between the will of the people and the rule of law, Americans were naturally receptive to the development of institutions that reflected each of these values separately. The legislature with its power to initiate programs and policies, to respond to the expressed interest of the public, embodied the doctrine of popular sovereignty. The courts, generally supposed to be without will as Hamilton said, generally revered as impartial and independent, fell heir almost by default to the guardianship of the fundamental law. It did not avail for Jeffersonian enemies of the judicial power to insist that a single department could exercise *both* the willing and the limiting functions. The bifurcation of the two values in the American mind impellingly suggested that the functions should be similarly separated. And the devotion of Americans to both popular sovereignty and fundamental law insured public support for the institution that represented each of them.

CONSEQUENCES FOR AMERICAN CONSTITUTIONALISM

This dualism of the American mind, symbolized on the one hand by "political" institutions like the Congress and the Presidency and on the other hand by the Court and the Constitu-

13

tion, helps account for a good deal that seems baffling in later history. In logical terms it might appear strange that the nation should resoundingly approve the New Deal in 1936 and a few months later stoutly defend against attack the Supreme Court that had cut the heart from the New Deal program. But the paradox is related as branch to root to the historic dualism between popular sovereignty and the doctrine of fundamental law that developed with the birth throes of the American political system. The separation of the two ideas in the American mind had been emphasized by intervening events: strong-minded judges had added new arguments for the Court's constitutional prerogative; congressmen and presidents, busy with more pressing concerns, had been content except for fitful rebellious impulses to let those arguments go unchallenged; and the cake of custom had hardened over the original disjunction. But it was made possible at the outset by our native tendency to harbor conflicting ideas without trying, or caring, to resolve them.

The United States began its history, then, with a Constitution that posed more questions than it answered and with a Supreme Court whose birthright was most uncertain. The temper of the times and the deep-seated inclinations of the American political character favored the future of both these institutions and at the same time prescribed their limits and helped determine their nature. American devotion to the principle of fundamental law gave the Constitution its odor of sanctity, and the American bent for evading contradictions by assigning values to separate compartments allowed the Supreme Court to assume the priestly mantle. But like most successes, in politics and elsewhere, this one had a price. The failure to resolve the conflict between popular sovereignty and fundamental law perhaps saved the latter principle, but by the same token it left the former intact. And this meant that the fundamental law could be enforced only within delicately defined boundaries, that constitutional law though not simply the creature of the popular will nevertheless had always to reckon with it, that the mandates of the Supreme Court must be shaped with an eye not only to legal right and wrong, but with an eye to what popular opinion would tolerate.

We have seen, then, that the Constitution makers postponed some of the most vital questions confronting them, that the Constitution and the Supreme Court inherited the quasi-religious symbolic quality attached to the doctrine of "higher law," but that the dogmas of popular sovereignty also continued to survive and flourish and therefore influence constitutionalism. The consequences of all this were several. For one thing the Constitution itself could not become the certain and immutable code of governmental conduct that some of its latter-day idolators imagined it to be. Conceived in ambiguity as well as liberty, it could never escape that legacy. The framers had said in effect: with respect to certain questions, some of them very momentous, the Constitution means whatever the circumstances of the future will allow it to mean. But since those circumstances were almost sure to vary, the result was that alterability became the law of the Constitution's being: it might mean one thing in 1855, something else in 1905, and something still different in 1955, depending upon what circumstances, including popular expectations, warranted.

To be sure, as the years went on there was a certain accumulation of fairly well-fixed interpretations, and the picture of a constitutional system in eternal flux should not be overdrawn. Some constitutional clauses are explicit enough (and frequently unimportant enough) so that argument about their meaning is improbable. It is unlikely that the states will ever be permitted to grant titles of nobility (Art. I, sec. 10); federal judges, once hired, can feel secure against direct wage cuts (Art. III, sec. 1). Other phrases often rather technical in nature, like the "ex post facto" clause (Art. I, sec. 10), seem to resist the winds of innovation more efficiently than others. Moreover, because the illusion of continuity must be respected, great constitutional changes are likely to come slowly. Nevertheless only a very bold constitutional scholar would declare that he *knows* how the commerce clause or the due process clauses will be understood by the next generation. And when we count up the clauses whose past is variable and whose future is uncertain they far exceed in significance if not in number their more stable fellows.

THE COURT'S CONSTITUTIONAL POWERS AND DUTIES

As for the Supreme Court, its nature has also been heavily and permanently influenced by the factors just described. As might be expected, any description of the judicial function in America is shot through with paradoxes. To begin with, the observer confronts the fact that the Court does inherit a responsibility for helping to guide the nation, especially with respect to those long-term "value questions" that are so vital to the maintenance of a just political order. A good many gallons of ink have been spilled over the issue of whether such a heavy assignment should have devolved on the judiciary. John Marshall, "the great Chief Justice," has been accused of seizing the bitter cup all too gladly and thus setting a pattern of usurpation for future judges to follow. Insofar as this indictment rests on the supposed "intent of the framers," it suffers from the weakness already remarked: that so few of the framers had any clear views one way or another about the subject.

On the other hand, insofar as the charge is that the nation was unwise to delegate this duty to the judges (or allow them to assume it), it may be right, but is also perilously near to irrelevance. For this amounts to saying that America was unwise to be the nation that it was. The American mind conceived a dichotomy between the willed law of legislative enactment and the discovered or pronounced law of the Constitution, and "judicial review" was, as we have seen, one result. The fallacy of making such a distinction may be palpable enough from our modern perspective, but the fact remains that it was not palpable to Marshall's generation, and nothing very helpful is accomplished by arguing that it should have been.

Nor is it much more profitable to urge that the Court should now put off the responsibility it once so eagerly took up, even if it be conceded that the original arrogation was unwise. Historical accident and bad logic may explain the inception of judicial review, but by now the American nation has lived with the consequences for more than 150 years. Our courts and, even more important, our legislatures have been shaped by the understanding that the judiciary will help in charting the path of governmental policy. A rough division of labor has developed from that understanding, for it is assumed that the legislature can focus largely on the task of "interest representation," while passing on to the courts a substantial share of the responsibility for considering the long-term constitutional questions that continually arise. Appearances may be deceptive. Congressmen may self-righteously insist that they serve both the Constitutional Tradition and their Constituents, but the needs of these two masters seem to coincide with remarkable invariability; and it is fair to infer that interests and pressures play the larger part in the legislative process.

Surely this is no indictment of that process, for the American tradition respects, as has been said, the will of today's popular majority, and interests must therefore be paid due heed. But the American tradition also sets great store, as we have also seen, by the set of values associated with the "rule of law," which history has rightly or wrongly consigned in heavy part to the judiciary. In a world of abstractions, one might argue that this historic division, since it defies good sense, ought to be obliterated. But in the world that history has given us, the almost certain result would be that pure calculation of interest-group pressures defined the course of government in the United States. It is too much to ask that a legislative process as interest-dominated as ours abjure its traditions at this late date and take on the functions of a high court as well. Yet until it does, the judiciary must accept its own traditional responsibility, lest the very idea of limited government be lost. Critics may legitimately debate whether the Court should play a greater or lesser part in directing the ship of state. That it must play some part is the penalty of its heritage.

THE CONDITIONS OF JUDICIAL CONTROL

Yet once this is said, it must immediately be added—or reiterated —that the tradition which transmits this power to the Court likewise prescribes the conditions of its exercise. The nation expects the judges to aid in deciding policy questions, but the nation is prone, with sublime inconsistency, to grow fiercely resentful if the aid becomes repression, if the judges bypass certain ill-marked but nevertheless quite real boundaries, two of which merit special consideration.

In the first place, there are the limitations implied by the fact that the Supreme Court is expected to be both a "court" in the orthodox sense of the word and something very much more as well. A full account of the confusions fostered by this seeming contradiction would almost involve a recapitulation of Supreme Court history. Legions of judges and their devotees have believed, or professed to believe, that constitutional law was a technical mystery revealing itself in terms of unmistakable precision to those who had the key, that the Constitution was the record and the judges merely the impartial phonograph that played it, a group of men who somehow managed to stop being men when they put on their robes and would not dream of letting their subjective value judgments affect their understanding of the Constitution. No court was ever like this, no system of law was ever so sure a guide to its interpreters. And the myth of a perfect judiciary perfectly administering a perfect Constitution was therefore deeply impaired in the twentieth century by writers who pointed out what some perceptive observers had always known—that judges are mortal. Like senators and presidents, it was said, judges may have prejudices, and those prejudices may affect their understanding of the Constitution. In fact, the critics went on, the American Supreme Court, so far from merely and imperturbably reflecting eternal constitutional verities, is a willing, policy-making, *political* body.

All this was perfectly true as far as it went, and it provided a useful antidote to previous oversimplifications. But the trouble was that it tended to foster an oversimplification of its own:

"legal realists," impressed by the discovery that the Supreme Court was more than a court, were sometimes prone to treat it as if it were not a court at all, as if its "courthood" were a pure façade for political functions indistinguishable from those performed by the legislature. Such a view bypasses everything that is really interesting about the institution and obscures, as much as the discredited old mythology ever did, its true nature.

For the fascinating thing about the Supreme Court has been that it blends orthodox judicial functions with policy-making functions in a complex mixture. And the Court's power is accounted for by the fact that the mixture is maintained in nice balance; but the fact that it *must* be maintained in such a balance accounts for the limitations of that power. The Court's claim on the American mind derives from the myth of an impartial, judicious tribunal whose duty it is to preserve our sense of continuity with the fundamental law. Because that law was initially stated in ambiguous terms, it has been the duty of the Court to make "policy decisions" about it, that is, to decide what it means in the circumstances existing when the question is presented. But though the judges do enter this realm of policy-making, they enter with their robes on, and they can never (or at any rate seldom) take them off; they are both empowered and restricted by their "courtly" attributes.

They cannot, for example, even decide a question unless it is presented in the form of a "case" between two or more interested parties; and the Supreme Court early, and wisely, held that to render "advisory opinions" even to the President would be incongruous with the judicial function. Sometimes the Court is criticized for leaning over backward to find technical and, to a layman, unduly "legalistic" reasons for leaving important constitutional questions unsettled. Often the drag of precedent inhibits the judges from revising constitutional principles as quickly as might be desirable. And finally there are whole large areas of constitutional determination which the Court deliberately and rather consistently leaves alone (for example, the issue of whether a state has "a republican form of government," Art. IV, sec. 4) on the grounds that the questions therein raised are not appropriate for judicial determination.

Any individual decision along any of these lines may well be subject to criticism, for the judges of the Supreme Court, being men, can err. But it is the greatest of nonsense to generalize the criticism into impatience with the Court's "legalistic" demeanor as such, since the logical conclusion of such a criticism is to align the judicial power squarely with the legislative power and to erase the differentiation of function that is the Court's basis for being. And it is also wrong to suppose that the Court's insistence on such attributes of judiciality is a mere pose, designed to hoodwink the public without hampering the judges. In certain spectacular cases in our history the Court has seemed to take leave of courtly procedures in order to remedy an injustice, real or fancied. Such a landmark of judicial temerity was the decision in 1895 which outlawed a national income tax, and no sophisticated student of the Court would deny that it can sometimes forget its "legalistic" trappings and can at other times refashion them to serve the judicial purpose of the moment. But in most cases such technical legal limitations do play a part that is not sham but perfectly real. The judges have usually known what students have sometimes not known—that their tribunal must be a court, as well as seem one, if it is to retain its power. The idea of fundamental law as a force in its own right, distinguishable from today's popular will, can only be maintained by a pattern of Court behavior that emphasizes the separation. If departures from that pattern are too frequent and too extreme, the emphasis will be lost and the idea itself will be imperiled.

One consequence, then, of the Supreme Court's peculiar origins is this necessity that it perform legislative (or quasi-legislative) tasks with judicial tools, which is roughly akin to the assignment of playing baseball with a billiard cue. But its problems do not end there. A second result, as has already been intimated, is the need for the judges to reckon, in making rules and guiding policy, with the imperatives of public opinion no matter how impeccably "judicial" is the method by which the rules are arrived at. This is not to say that the Court should consult the latest bulletins on the popular climate and shape its judgments accordingly. But it is to say that public concurrence sets an outer boundary for judicial policy-making; that judicial ideas of the good society can never be too far removed from the popular ideas. The Republic might have been dedicated at the outset to the principle of pure popular sovereignty, and in that event the Supreme Court would have inherited only the important but secondary responsibility of statutory interpretation. On the other hand, it is imaginatively, though not perhaps practically, conceivable to establish a governmental system in which the fundamental law absolutely controls the public will, and in such a system the Court might enjoy utter independence. But America, as we have seen, chose neither of these worlds, but tried to have the best of them both: the upshot is that the Court, while sometimes checking or at any rate modifying the popular will, is itself in turn checked or modified.

America has thus had two sovereigns, but this somewhat outlandish arrangement has been maintained only because each of the partners has known the meaning of self-restraint. In the critical literature of the past generation or two, one has read much about judicial tyranny, and the vision of a populace bent on social reform but shackled by an unfeeling Court's despotism seems to have beguiled more than one observer. In truth the Supreme Court has seldom, if ever, flatly and for very long resisted a really unmistakable wave of public sentiment. It has worked with the premise that constitutional law, like politics itself, is a science of the possible.

THE CONTOURS OF COURT HISTORY

There is a final point, which is at the same time very much like a summary of the discussion so far. We have seen that both the meaning of the Constitution and the nature of the Supreme Court's authority were left in doubt by the framers, that circumstances nonetheless conspired to favor the early growth of both constitutionalism and judicial power, but that those same circumstances also helped to set the terms within which these institutions would develop. The Constitution became a symbol of American patriotic devotion, but a symbol whose continued force depended on its continued flexibility in the face of shifting national needs. The Supreme Court became a venerated institution, half judicial tribunal and half political preceptor, sensitive but not subservient to popular expectations, obliged by its tradition to share the duties of statesmanship, but equally obliged to be alert that its share did not exceed its capacities.

The history of the Court and its treatment of the Constitution can be broadly understood as an endless search for a position in American government that is appropriate to these conditions imposed by its genesis. The quest is laden with difficulties because the paradoxes of the Court's existence can only be reconciled, even temporarily, by the most delicate balancing of judgments. It is unending because every such tentative reconciliation is sure to be disturbed ultimately by the relentless course of history, and every such major disturbance sends the judges forth on another chapter in their odyssey.

In each chapter certain dominant judicial interests take form, certain dominant values emerge, and the Court can be observed struggling to formulate a judicial role that will reinforce those interests and values within the subtle limits of judicial capability. We need not pause just now over the issue of whether these preoccupations and postures are consciously chosen, nor need we trouble ourselves that individual judges may vary in the degree of their conformity to the pattern, except insofar as this may affect the pattern itself. The refinements of the judicial motivation process are intriguing to be sure, but too much concern with them may cause an observer to miss the broad trends that give meaning to an epoch in constitutional history. Conceding that there are variations within the framework, we can nevertheless identify three great periods in American constitutional development: 1789 to the close of the Civil War; 1865 to the "Court revolution" of 1937; and 1937 to the present. The judicial interests and values that characterize each period are sufficiently articulated to be significant; and the Court's struggle to define its role as great new historical movements alter the backdrop, supplies a further element of dramatic change and uncertainty. If the framers had tried to settle all "constitutional" questions that confronted them; if they had even assumed the more modest task of specifically circumscribing the judicial power; if the doctrine of legislative supremacy had been a little more firmly intrenched in 1789; if judges like

Marshall had been a little more inclined toward abnegation and a little less inclined toward politics, the uncertainties would be very different, the tale would be of another order. But then the country it was told about would not be the historical United States.

II

The Establishment of the Right
To Decide: 1789-1810

Americans have always experienced a peculiar difficulty in accommodating themselves to one of the least contestable observations made in the preceding chapter—that the Supreme Court is a wilful, policy-making agency of American government. In the long and crowded history of antijudicial polemics the most persistent angry charge has been that the Court, in this situation or that, has been guided by its prepossessions rather than by the unambiguous mandates of the fundamental law. On the other hand, the defenders of the Court in such debates (that is, those who approve the policy decisions in question) have ordinarily and with indignation rejected this impeachment, insisting that the judges were the helpless instruments of constitutional logic. Since the combatants have a bewildering way of shifting sides from year to year or at any rate from decade to decade, a watcher of the constitutional skies might draw a somewhat puzzling conclusion—that for many Americans the Court is the echo of the Constitution when it agrees with them and the voice of subjective prejudice when it does not.

The effect of this musical chairs game is unfortunately to obscure any coherent view of what the Court is really up to at any given time. Those who like the Court's record in that time are indisposed to admit that it is up to anything except its mythic business of consulting the oracle; and those who disapprove its record are too wrathful over the current usurpation to offer reliable judgments.

Nevertheless it is perfectly apparent to the detached observer that the Court's decisions do tend to fall into patterns that reflect current judicial views of what ought to be done; and that these views, though heavily influenced by the nature of the forum that issues them, are nonetheless policy determinations. The very question of what subjects should claim judicial attention, involves an avowed or implicit decision about what is most important in the American polity at any given time, for the Court has always enjoyed some leeway in controlling its own jurisdiction (though less in the past than it does now). The Court's "interests" are likely indeed to be affected by the historical context, but historical imperatives can be strengthened or weakened by the Court's eagerness or reluctance to accede to them. And since the constitutional questions that do successfully claim the attention of the Court are often those least answerable by rules of thumb, the predilections, the "values" of the judges, must play a part in supplying answers to them.

From 1789 until the Civil War, the dominant interest of the Supreme Court was in that greatest of all the questions left unsolved by the founders—the nation-state relationship. And the dominant judicial value, underlying the drift of decision in widely different areas, was the value of preserving the American

Union. To be sure, the judges of the Supreme Court were not entirely single-minded and so of course other interests, other values, intruded upon the judicial mind and clamored for attention. Marshall and, indeed, the American bench and bar in general, were deeply concerned over the question of property rights, and it is possible to interpret the decisions of the Marshall court in terms that emphasize this preoccupation. Early in Taney's era Jacksonian distrust of finance capitalism found expression in judicial decisions; later the issue of slavery ran its dark course through constitutional law. Such matters as these profoundly engaged the judges' interests, and there is no disposition here to minimize the part they played in shaping legal doctrine or to deny that in isolated cases that part might be the crucial one.

But the question of nation-state relationships was in this era so closely entwined with such issues as property rights and slavery that to touch one was to touch the other, and we can be sure that it was never far from the judges' minds even when they seemed for the moment to be focusing on something else. And the motive of preserving the Union is persistently suggested by decision after decision, the one factor that makes sense out of apparent doctrinal inconsistencies, the often-inarticulate major premise that binds even such disparate spirits as Marshall and Taney together in a common cause.

It is hardly surprising that this should be so considering the drift of American history during the period, the evasiveness of the Constitution on these points, and the extremely tentative nature of the Court's own status. The states' rights and nationalist fetishes were the great herrings across the trail of American politics. Where reason and prudence were arrayed against him, a partisan could always invoke the dogma of states' rights or national sovereignty and feel fairly confident that tempers would rise and good sense depart. The nation lived in a nearly constant alternation of fears that it would cease being a nation altogether or become too much of one. And the Constitution alone could not serve to quiet these misgivings, for, as the warring camps soon discovered, it could be cited on either side, depending on whether a "strict construction" or a "loose construction" were adopted.

These ubiquitous questions thus inhered in almost every constitutional case the Supreme Court faced. At the same time, the Court's very title to decide them depended upon the Union's preservation, and this made it almost sure that the judges would put that value first. Hamilton hoped to strengthen the nation by giving capitalism a stake in its survival. Whatever the failures of that particular program, just such a marriage of interest and principle was accomplished by the establishment of the federal judiciary.

Within this broad category of interests then and with this dominant value of unionism for guidance, the Supreme Court of the pre–Civil War years sought to define its role. The relevant query for the judges—as for a student of the period—was not whether the Union ought to be maintained and made "more perfect"; there was all but unanimous agreement about that. The problem was how the Court could most usefully serve the cause it had espoused, or, to put it in another way, what view of the Constitution was best calculated to preserve the Union— and thereby the Supreme Court.

With the advantage of hindsight we can see that the judges had three major "role problems" before them. In the first place they must establish, not merely in theory but in practice as well, the doctrine of *judicial independence*. It is true that this doctrine was well rooted in colonial tradition and that the framers had tried to implement it by providing life tenure during "good behavior" for federal judges and by prohibiting reduction of their salaries. But it is also true that Congress was given powers, such as impeachment and control of the appellate jurisdiction, which were quite adequate to obliterate judicial independence if Congress were determined to do so.

Second, the Court must gain acceptance for the idea that among the powers thus independently exercised was that of *judicial review*, that is, the power to refuse to enforce an unconstitutional act of either the state or national government. And finally that power itself must be nourished and cultivated so that it will grow into the doctrine of *judicial sovereignty*, or the idea that a law may be held unconstitutional if the Court thinks it is, even though the case is not plain, and that the Court's opinion to this effect is binding on other branches of government. These problems need not be met in just this order; they need not be resolved with absolute finality. But they must be dealt with and partially answered if the Supreme Court is to play a significant part in the long struggle to preserve the Union.

YOUTHFUL UNCERTAINTIES

It is hard for a student of judicial review to avoid feeling that American constitutional history from 1789 to 1801 was marking time. The great shadow of John Marshall, who became Chief Justice in the latter year, falls across our understanding of that first decade; and it has therefore the quality of a play's opening moments with minor characters exchanging trivialities while they and the audience await the appearance of the star.

Such an impression is not altogether unjustified. The Supreme

The Establishment of the Right To Decide

Court was, as we have seen, uncertain of its standing in those early years. When John Jay refused to resume the chief justice-ship in 1801, he told President Adams that he had no faith the Court could acquire enough "energy, weight and dignity" to play a salient part in the nation's affairs. Each justice was burdened with the ridiculous chore of riding circuit, turning up twice a year to attend circuit court in each of four or five federal districts, which meant that judicial energies were dissipated in endless travel under the semiprimitive conditions of the day. Several statesmen of distinction like Edmund Pendleton of Virginia and Charles Cotesworth Pinckney of South Carolina refused appointment to the Court, and several more resigned in favor of greener pastures, including two Chief Justices, John Jay and Oliver Ellsworth. Few cases came to the Court compared with the torrents of later years, and even fewer were very important. Not one decision holding a state or federal law unconstitutional was handed down. And in most of the cases that were decided the practice of delivering opinions *seriatim* (a separate opinion by each judge) diffused the impact of the judgments and made it all the less likely that the Court would be regarded as an equal partner in the federal triumvirate.

Of course constitutional questions were arising. It would have been strange if they had not in these years when the Constitution itself was being tried on for size. But for the time being most of them were fought out in the legislative branches, in cabinet meetings, or in the forum of public opinion. The first Congress, acting in accord with the conditions attached to ratification by several of the states, proposed twelve amendments, ten of which were ultimately ratified and became the "Bill of Rights." The bill to incorporate a national bank raised the grave question of whether the national government's authority should be broadly or strictly construed, for no such incorporation power was specifically granted in the Constitution. Madison in Congress and Jefferson in the cabinet sharply opposed the proposal, arguing for strict construction, while Hamilton's astute defense of the broader viewpoint not only won the day but became one of the great state papers of American history. The issue was not to reach the Supreme Court for almost thirty years.

Even when the rod of power was explicitly offered, the judiciary displayed some reluctance about grasping it. Certain ticklish questions of international law were arising in connection with the Neutrality Proclamation of 1793, and although President Washington wanted the Court's advice in solving them, the Court declined to give him any, arguing that "advisory opinions" were inconsistent with the judicial function. And somewhat earlier, when Congress had tried to invest the judiciary with authority to settle claims of invalid war veterans, two Supreme Court justices sitting on the circuit court joined a district judge in modestly rejecting the assignment. The law, they declared, is unconstitutional, because "the business directed by this act is not of a judicial nature" (first *Hayburn* case). All this suggests a Court bypassed in the major power-struggles of the day and by no means eager to have greatness thrust upon it.

But this does not mean that the Court of the 1790's was unmindful of its potential as a factor in American government. In fact, as the *Hayburn* case suggests, the judges were quietly laying the groundwork of power even while power itself was allowed to slip away, were preparing for a time when great matters, such as the issue of the Bank, would come within the judicial purview. The refusal to perform "non-judicial" functions reflected a shrewd insight—that the Court's position would ultimately depend on preserving its difference from the other branches of government. The Congress and the presidency would always have roots in the power structure of American society, while the Court must find its support in the popular belief that the judiciary stands apart and defends the fundamental law. And the decision in *Hayburn*, with all its appearance of self-denial, was bold enough in other respects: it rested on the cardinal premise that the judiciary could disregard a legislative act which it believed was unconstitutional.

That premise, the very essence of the Court's future greatness, was taking vague but perceptible shape throughout these years. Hamilton had supplied an invaluable cue in the *Federalist Papers* by flatly claiming such a power for the judiciary; and those papers were already becoming a venerated source of constitutional guidance. State court judges were following his lead from time to time, asserting their right to determine the validity of state laws in the light of the state constitutions. The members of the Supreme Court themselves, not only in *Hayburn* but in other cases, were giving voice to the idea of judicial review in ways that allowed them to avoid being called to account for all the idea's implications. Justice Paterson indulged in 1795 in some high-sounding language about the judicial duty to declare unwarranted legislative acts void; but the occasion was a jury charge in the course of circuit court proceedings, and it was not at all clear that the doctrine he enunciated had any practical effect on the outcome of the case. In several other cases, decided by the Supreme Court, the justices quite evidently assumed in their opinions that they *could* set unconstitutional state or federal laws aside, but they elected in these circumstances not to do so. This approach had the double advantage of disarming critics concerned with the outcome of the immediate cause and at the same time adding a brick or two to the edifice of precedent on which the judicial future would depend.

Nor was the Court of this era as neglectful of the nation-state relationship problem as its failure to hold a state act unconstitutional might suggest. In fact, its first real foray into hotly disputed constitutional realms indicated zeal and audacity somewhat in advance of the times. In the course of the ratification controversy, more than one apprehensive Antifederalist had noticed the phrase in Article III which extended the judicial power to controversies "between a State and citizens of another State," and had darkly suspected that it might be invoked to subvert state sovereignty. Did the clause mean that an individual could sue a state in the federal courts? So it might seem from the language alone, but the Constitution's defenders, including Madison, Hamilton, and Marshall, rejected the inference and soothed this fear of its detractors: no state, they said, would be haled into federal courts under the authority of this clause, for the sovereign is not subject to suit. Now however, in 1793, the Supreme Court chose to think otherwise. When two citizens of South Carolina brought an action against Georgia for the recovery of debt and Georgia refused to appear in her own defense, the Court declared that states were suable and rendered judgment for the plaintiff.

The practical consequences of this doctrine were grave enough, for the states had been playing fast and loose in fiscal matters for years; and the doctrine, if enforced, might expose them to harassment by a swarm of creditors. But, even worse, the theoretical premise of the decision was an outright challenge to state sovereignty. The judges had forthrightly recognized that they were being asked to make their first great decision about the nature of the Union and had held, in the words of Justice Wilson, that *"as to the purposes of the Union,* therefore, *Georgia is not a sovereign state."* The point seems sensible and indeed almost inevitable if the Union was to have meaning, but 1793 was too soon to state it so baldly. A gale of opposition at once arose from all sides, and a constitutional amendment denying that states were suable in federal courts by citizens of other states, was proposed and later ratified (Amendment XI). The larger question of the nature of the Union was postponed for the more devious talents of Marshall to cope with. The pre-Marshall justices had made two mistakes their great successor usually managed to avoid: in their ardor to establish an ultra-Federalist doctrine they had spoken overplainly; and they had spoken thus in support of a doctrine that immediately imperiled the concrete interests of most of the states. The resulting united protest was too strong for the Court's nascent independence to withstand, and the judges' fingers were badly (though not fatally) singed.

As *Chisholm* v. *Georgia* suggests, then, the pre-Marshall Court was fully conscious that its greatest problem was the nation-state relationship, and it was heavily disposed to create, or to encourage the creation of, a consolidated national union. And as tentative gropings toward a doctrine of judicial review suggest, the Court was also perfectly aware that it could carry out this imposing assignment only if it possessed final authority to decide questions of constitutionality. Why then did it not proceed at once to undermine state sovereignty and to assert the full range of the judicial prerogative? Why, for example, did the Court allow more than a decade to pass without directly invalidating a state law on constitutional grounds? Why are the statements of the doctrine of judicial review artfully concealed in innocuous decisions or pronounced so equivocally as to leave the whole matter in doubt?

In part the answer is that the judges understood, whether consciously or instinctively, their limitations as well as their opportunities. They realized that the Constitution did not explicitly accord them the power they coveted and that public opinion had not yet filled in this gap in the organic law. They realized that the characteristically unqualified logic of Hamilton, however convincing and tempting it might seem, was not quite apt for their purposes. The essayist Hamilton could sweep premises, argument, and conclusions together in a single brave statement at a single moment in time. The constitutional judge —or the would-be constitutional judge—needed time as an ally and could not afford to treat it so cavalierly. The judicial empire, if there was to be one, had to be conquered slowly, piece by piece. An idea could be implied today, obliquely stated tomorrow, and flatly asserted the next day. But months and years had to pass before the judiciary was ready to give that idea fully effective life as a principle of decision. Meanwhile the forthright logic of Hamilton was being transmuted into the less tidy but more potent logic of public consent, as the original idea worked its way into the consciousness of educated Americans. And then, when the moment for real action came, the ground might be ready.

THE MENACE OF JEFFERSON AND THE CAUTION OF MARSHALL

The ground might indeed have been ready in 1800 if the nicely ordered political world of the Federalists' dreams had behaved itself as they thought they had a right to expect. The Court, as we have seen, had laid the basis for judicial review in its pronouncements of the past ten years. The idea was now familiar to most of those who thought about such matters, and there is no reason to believe that many of them staunchly opposed it. Neither, to be sure, is there evidence that they fully understood its implications as a doctrine of judicial *supremacy*, or expected that the Court would use its veto in any but a clear case; but some of those implications could wait a bit longer for the future to unfold them. Judicial nationalism had been set back on its heels by the reaction to the *Chisholm* case, but in 1796 the Court had dealt state sovereignty an almost equally grievous blow when it held that the peace treaty with Great Britain overrode state laws affecting the rights of British creditors, and the reaction had not been disastrous, however ill-tempered. The judiciary's time for greatness might have seemed at hand.

But the world of politics chose this moment to display a mind of its own. The Federalists, in a fine frenzy engendered partly by fear of France and partly by well-founded doubts about their own ability to hold the American electorate's support, had passed the Alien and Sedition Acts in 1798. The judges of the federal bench were almost to a man ardent Federalist partisans, and they had enthusiastically shouldered the task of enforcing the Sedition Act, which was designed, among other things, to visit savage punishment on those who criticized the national administration. Supreme Court justices like Paterson, Iredell, and above all Samuel Chase earned the hatred of Jefferson's fast-growing Republican party, not only by presiding over the convictions of men who had called John Adams names ("hoary headed incendiary") and otherwise maligned Federalism, but by revealing on the bench a vengeful partisanship that rekindled pre-Revolutionary memories of the king's courts. Insult was added to injury when federal judges undertook, even without benefit of a statute, to punish under the English common law those who violated Washington's Neutrality Proclamation or the Treaty of Peace with Great Britain. Justice Chase, not content with giving partisan speeches from the bench, openly and eagerly participated in political campaigns against the monstrous threat of Jeffersonianism.

This would have been a bad sort of game for the judiciary to play under any circumstances, but in light of the political realities of the time it was almost suicidal. The Alien and Sedition Acts called forth the Kentucky and Virginia resolutions which challenged, in language composed by Jefferson and Madison, respectively, the whole doctrine of national supremacy and unity upon which the very existence of the Supreme Court hinged. The party of Jefferson won the election of 1800, and the victors came to office with an understandably bitter distrust of the national judiciary which had so eagerly joined in the persecution of Republicans. The outgoing Federalists did their part to make a bad situation worse by passing the Judiciary Act of 1801, creating a number of new federal judgeships which were hastily filled by Adams, and reducing the number of Supreme Court justices from six to five. This law was not without merits, but those merits were forgotten in the justifiable Republican anger at its obvious partisanship. The Federalists, having lost the other two branches of government, hoped to maintain their control nonetheless by intrenching a pro-Federalist judiciary protected by life tenure.

It is little wonder that the noble rage of Jefferson's party, once focused on the task of winning a national election, was now directed at the federal judiciary and its head and symbol, the Supreme Court. When Adams, as one of the last acts of his administration, appointed the Federalist John Marshall to the

The Establishment of the Right To Decide

Chief Justiceship, the Republicans felt they had endured enough such Parthian salvos and began to map out a counter-campaign of their own. The Judiciary Act of 1801 was repealed only a little more than a year after its passage, notwithstanding Federalist cries that the repealing act was itself unconstitutional. John Adams' "midnight appointments" of new federal judges were thus for the most part wiped away. As for the remaining members of the federal (and Federalist) bench, the awful power of impeachment was to be invoked: the judiciary must bow to the will of the people—which was, of course, in Jeffersonian theory the will of the Republicans—or be turned out. The principle of judicial independence was faced with its first great challenge.

This threat to judicial independence loomed over the Marshall Court during the first few years of his incumbency and inevitably conditioned what might be called the strategy of judicial behavior. Marshall desired as much as Wilson or Jay had, to establish the power of the judiciary on solid ground and to use the power to defend the cause of national union. Their Court had in its first few years prepared the way for this and was proceeding gradually but surely along that way when the Jeffersonian tempest, generated in part by the judiciary's own folly, burst forth. As a result of it, Marshall's opportunity was perilously difficult for him to grasp, and in fact the great day when the Court would declare a state law unconstitutional was postponed for almost another full decade. Not until then, or nearly then, was it clear that localist sentiment in the American body politic was less robust than he had feared it was. Not until then did he know that judicial prestige was durable enough to warrant some risks, that judicial independence was at least relatively secure. Not until then did the Court begin to be a major factor in American government.

Important as Marshall is in the history of American jurisprudence, it is not his appointment that marks the Court's coming of age, for the Court, like an individual, grew up slowly. Marshall did establish almost at once the custom of letting one justice's opinion, usually his own, stand for the decision of the whole Court, and this custom gave the judicial pronouncements a forceful unity they had formerly lacked. But in spite of this the Court after 1801 was for some time no more formidable than it had been before; judicial independence had not yet been firmly established; the real bite of the doctrine of judicial review had not yet made itself felt; the problem of the Union was still comparatively untouched. Marshall was holding back, awaiting a more propitious future. His pre-eminence among builders of the American constitutional tradition rests not only on his well-known boldness, his "tiger instinct for the jugular vein" as an enthusiastic metaphorist once called it, but also on his less-noticed sense of self-restraint.

The famous case *Marbury* v. *Madison* in 1803 appears to contradict this proposition but in fact confirms it. The decision is a masterwork of indirection, a brilliant example of Marshall's capacity to sidestep danger while seeming to court it, to advance in one direction while his opponents are looking in another.

In its closing hours the Adams administration had done its competent best, as we have seen, to fill up federal offices with loyal anti-Jeffersonians. But events were moving rapidly, some details were apt to be neglected, and when Jefferson took over, the commission of one William Marbury to be Justice of the Peace in the District of Columbia had not been delivered to him, though it had been signed and sealed. The new President was indisposed to mend this oversight of his predecessors, so

The Establishment of the Right To Decide

Marbury asked the Supreme Court for a writ which would compel Jefferson's Secretary of State, Madison, to hand over the commission. This created what seemed a painful and unpromising dilemma for Marshall and his Court. If they upheld Marbury and ordered delivery of the commission, the order would surely be ignored by Madison, the Court would be exposed as impotent to enforce its mandates, the shakiness of judicial prestige would be dramatically emphasized. If on the other hand they did not uphold Marbury, they would give aid and comfort to Jefferson and might seem to support his denunciation of the "midnight appointments." The latter course was impossibly distasteful to an ardently Federalist bench; the former was humiliating and might well be risky.

But Marshall was equal to the occasion. Marbury's commission, he said, is being illegally withheld from him by the Jeffersonian administration and a writ can appropriately be directed to a cabinet official when he fails his duty. However, the Supreme Court is not the proper tribunal to supply Marbury with a remedy in this case, for the Court does not possess the power to issue writs in cases of this kind. It is true that Section 13 of the Judiciary Act of 1789 seems to grant the Court such power, but that provision is itself invalid. For the Court's original jurisdiction is defined in the Constitution, and a congressional act like this one, which adds to the original jurisdiction, is therefore unconstitutional. And an unconstitutional law is void and must be so treated by the Supreme Court. Mr. Marbury then must look elsewhere for redress of his just grievance—with the Court's best wishes.

A more adroit series of parries and ripostes would be difficult to imagine. The danger of a head-on clash with the Jeffersonians was averted by the denial of jurisdiction; but, at the same time, the declaration that the commission was illegally withheld scotched any impression that the Court condoned the administration's behavior. These negative maneuvers were artful achievements in their own right. But the touch of genius is evident when Marshall, not content with having rescued a bad situation, seizes the occasion to set forth the doctrine of judicial review. It is easy for us to see in retrospect that the occasion was golden. The attention of the Republicans was focused on the question of Marbury's commission, and they cared very little how the Court went about justifying a hands-off policy so long as that policy was followed. Moreover, the Court was in the delightful position, so common in its history but so confusing to its critics, of rejecting and assuming power in a single breath, for the Congress had tried here to give the judges an authority they could not constitutionally accept and the judges were high-mindedly refusing. The moment for immortal statement was at hand all right, but only a judge of Marshall's discernment could have recognized it.

As for the statement itself, it exemplifies the gift for argumentative effectiveness, the masterful sense of strategy, that is illustrated in Marshall's whole approach to the case and was perhaps his supreme talent. He was able to endow his arguments with the flavor of the irresistible through a combination of lucidity and self-confidence:

The question of whether an Act repugnant to the Constitution can become the law of the land, is a question deeply interesting to the United States; but, happily, not of an intricacy proportioned to its interest. It seems only necessary to recognize certain principles, supposed to have been long and well-established, to decide it.

Marshall then proceeds to an examination of those principles for the benefit of the few who might not realize how "long and well-established" they were. These hypothetical adversaries are chosen with great care—they are evidently those who would deny the power of judicial review *altogether*. Imagine a law that clearly violates the Constitution, says Marshall, for example, a duty on state exports explicitly violating Article I, section 9. Surely the judges are not bound to enforce such an act, to treat it as valid. Now many, though not all, of Marshall's listeners would probably concede this point as far as it goes; the real questions for them would arise when the statute was not a *clear* violation of the Constitution, or when judges purported to speak on constitutional questions not only for themselves but for the other branches as well, to presume that the judicial finding of invalidity was final. These queries are not met at all in the argument of the *Marbury* case, and by ignoring them Marshall succeeds in beclouding them. Attacks on the discretionary scope and the finality of judicial review are henceforth confused with attacks on the minimal power Marshall here contends for, and the attackers thus find that though they aim for the weakest point in the judicial armor they almost invariably hit the strongest. The *Marbury* argument is justly celebrated, but not the least of its virtues is the fact that it is somewhat beside the point.

The *Marbury* opinion then is far from suggesting that Marshall was rash or even very bold in exercising judicial supervision at this stage of his career as Chief Justice. The decision was criticized for its dictum that the executive *could* be called to account by judicial process, but since the requested writ was in fact denied, no really great heat was generated even on this point. And as for the argument for judicial review, at the time only the Federalists paid much attention to it, and they of course were warmly approving; the Jeffersonians shed few tears over the voiding of a law that had been passed by Federalists in the first place.

The decision does suggest, however, that Marshall, though choosing the path of discretion in the immediate occasion, did not for a moment forget the long-term objectives—enhancement of judicial power in general and diminution of state autonomy in particular. The relevance of the *Marbury* case to the struggle against state autonomy is easy to miss, because the Chief Justice's specific target is a national statute. But the argument for holding an unconstitutional law void is phrased in very broad terms, and it applies equally whether the enacting body is Congress or a state legislature. In fact two of Marshall's three argumentative illustrations of obviously invalid laws would be just as apposite if state, rather than national, power were being called into question. The important point is that the Court may refuse to enforce an unconstitutional law, whatever its source may be. *Marbury* is thus not, as it might appear at first glance, a digression from the long-run struggle against excessive localism; on the contrary, it is a crucial skirmish in that campaign, for when state laws are later judicially challenged, the precedent of *Marbury* stands ready to back up the challenge.

THE ORDEAL OF JOHN MARSHALL; THE IMPEACHMENT
THREAT SUBSIDES

Meanwhile, however, the antijudicial brew of the Republicans was simmering and Marshall was constrained to adhere to the course of measured caution that *Marbury* represents. No one knew better than he that the ambitious assertions of that case would be quite meaningless in the face of concerted political resistance from the other branches, and he had no wish to provoke more united opposition than he already faced. In 1803, the very year of the *Marbury* decision, the Congress proceeded to the impeachment of John Pickering, Judge of the United States Court for the District of New Hampshire. This unfortunate man was hopelessly insane and a drunkard; his behavior on the bench for three years had been picturesquely irrational. There was no doubt that he now lacked the capacity to discharge the duties of office, but the Constitution provides no method for removal except "Impeachment for, and Conviction of, Treason, Bribery, or other high Crimes and Misdemeanors" (Art. II, sec. 4). Could a man who was clearly out of his mind and therefore not responsible be convicted of "high Crimes and Misdemeanors"? If not, could he be impeached?

The answer of the Republicans was to offer a theory of the impeachment power that would transcend such technical limits. As Senator Giles of Virginia was to put it: "Impeachment is nothing more than the enquiry, by the two Houses of Congress, whether the office of any public man might not be better filled by another. . . . A trial and removal of a judge need not imply any criminality or corruption in him." Pickering was convicted of high crimes and misdemeanors in spite of the legal anomaly this involved, the broad theory of the impeachment power being clearly implicit in the finding. But the principal interest of the theory's framers was not of course its first demented victim. Having given the idea a trial run, they now proposed to apply it to Samuel Chase of the Supreme Court, their particular bête noire among Federalist judges, and then to any other judicial menace to Republican aims, including John Marshall.

If the program had succeeded, the doctrine of an independent judiciary would have foundered and the whole future history of the Court might have been profoundly altered. Marshall's alarm can hardly be exaggerated. Apparently despairing of the chances for full independence, he privately suggested that Congress might be given appellate jurisdiction over Supreme Court decisions, as an alternative to impeachment. As a biographer remarks, we could not credit that Marshall ever subscribed to such an extraordinary notion if it had not been set forth in his own hand and the letter preserved. But the suggestion is a measure of his fear for his precious tribunal, of his conviction that a formal surrender of final authority might be the price that had to be paid in order to preserve any authority at all.

But the program did not succeed; it turned out that a lesser price would serve the purpose. The House, under the whip of the malignant John Randolph, duly brought impeachment articles against Chase, charging him with misconduct in the sedition trials of Fries and Callender in 1800, in his treatment of a grand jury at Newcastle in the same year, and in his political harangue of another grand jury in Baltimore in 1803. However, in conducting the impeachment proceedings before the Senate, Randolph and his cohorts seemed unable to decide whether to rest their case on charges of criminality or on the radical Republican theory that Congress could impeach merely for conduct it disapproved. The former charges were hard to prove, especially in the face of the formidable legal counsel that had assembled on Chase's behalf; yet the latter theory might well not receive the support of the necessary two-thirds of the Senate, and the whole cause might thus be lost. Instead of resolving this dilemma, the impeachers mingled criminality and mere objectionable conduct in a hopeless tangle. Those who might have supported one kind of charge were repelled by the other, and the Senate ended by finding Chase not guilty.

Mismanagement by the impeachment leaders undoubtedly contributed to this result. But the essential explanation is that many members of the Senate, including some Republicans, were not yet incensed enough with the judiciary to vote to destroy its independence. And their wrath was moderate or non-existent because the Court under Marshall had really done so little to incite it. The charge that the judiciary was tyrannically imposing a Federalist will on a Republican-minded nation did not square with the immediate facts of judicial behavior, whatever suspicions might be entertained about Marshall's long-term aspirations. And this impression of a non-aggressive bench had been further confirmed when, only a few days after *Marbury*, the Supreme Court sustained the validity of the law repealing the Judiciary Act of 1801. A Court that would pass up an opportunity to strike at this law, which all good Federalists regarded as the acme of Republican wickedness, could hardly be thought of as a despotic monster.

The failure of the Chase impeachment is one of the signal events in the history of the federal judiciary, because it set a precedent against loose construction of the impeachment power and thus supported the doctrine of judicial independence. And the price paid for this benign result was not the great one Marshall had feared—the vesting of an appellate authority in Congress—but simply a measure of present judicial self-restraint. Throughout the nation's future history this lesson can be read again and again: paradoxical though it may seem, the Supreme Court often gains rather than loses power by adopting a policy of forbearance.

The American Supreme Court

Marshall at any rate continued to take this lesson to heart for some years after Chase was saved from martyrdom. Of course it was by no means as clear to Marshall and his contemporaries as it is to us that impeachment was no longer an omnipresent danger. After his only real clash with Jefferson's administration, the trial of Aaron Burr for treason in 1807, demands for impeachment were heard once more. In this case Marshall seems to have been provoked by the partisan heat of the moment and by his hatred of Jefferson to depart from the pathway of caution. His interpretation of the treason clause of the Constitution made it quite impossible for Jefferson's administration to convict Burr, and his vulnerability to the consequent Republican attacks might appear all the greater when we reflect that the interpretation was of very doubtful validity.

But this time the antijudicial crusade, though extremely noisy, got nowhere at all. No doubt its progress was to a degree thwarted by the administration's involvement in other concerns, for the War of 1812 was already impending. But surely it can also be inferred that the doctrine of judicial independence had itself become a formidable shield against partisan assaults. The fact that the doctrine was now established and recognized did not mean that the judiciary was henceforth free of any threats from the congressional side. Under sufficient provocation the weapon of impeachment might yet be called into use, and in any event the less drastic but formidable power to restrict appellate jurisdiction was still untried. Henceforward Marshall and his cohorts could feel sure that such antijudicial action would not be undertaken lightly, that the Supreme Court's prestige was a factor to be reckoned with. In those first few stormy years of the Republic's history, the members of Congress and of the executive department had demonstrated over and over that the Constitution was less important to them than were political results. The records of both parties were strewn with evidence of this, but the Federalists' Sedition Act and the Jeffersonians' Louisiana Purchase are enough to illustrate the point. The judiciary had thus been left free to claim the Constitution for its own, to identify its own prestige with the prestige of fundamental law, and Marshall, with his happy combination of audacity and discretion, had made the most of the advantage.

Now at last then, after the reverberations of the Burr incident had subsided, Marshall was ready to follow the course which the judicial maneuvers of the past had made possible. He was ready to declare a state law unconstitutional, to show how the judiciary's carefully nurtured power and prestige could be employed to help preserve the Union.

The case, *Fletcher* v. *Peck* in 1810, involved the notorious Yazoo land-grant scandal. The details of this outrageous but fascinating affair are too intricate to be traced here; a good, long story must be shortened unmercifully. In 1795, Georgia had sold at a bargain price a huge tract of land comprising most of the modern states of Alabama and Mississippi. It quickly became known that all but one of the members of the legislature who voted for the sale had been bribed to do so, and a newly elected legislature, inflamed with righteous indignation, hastened to rescind the grant. However, before this virtuous step could be taken, the original purchasers had resold millions of acres of the land to supposedly innocent third parties, and the question of their titles' validity now came before the Supreme

Court. The argument was that the rescinding act was a violation of the Constitution and that the third-party titles were therefore still sound.

John Marshall and a unanimous Court agreed. The rescinding act was invalid and must be held so by the Supreme Court; this much was clear. But the exact basis for the holding was far from clear, for Marshall seemed reluctant to rest his judgment on one ground alone, probably because of the lingering difficulties each argument separately presented.

At one point he seemed to declare explicitly that the rescinding act impaired the obligation of contracts in violation of Article I, section 10, of the Constitution. But this declaration encountered two serious objections: that the contract clause was probably meant to apply to contracts between private individuals and not between the state and individuals; and that in any event a grant is not a contract carrying an obligation. Marshall met both of these hazards and purported to dispose of them, but we may doubt that he was fully confident he had done so.

At another point he intimated that the Georgia act was a violation of the ex post facto clause, but the trouble here was that the clause had been held applicable only to criminal legislation some twelve years before, and the law now in question of course concerned purely civil matters. At still another point he suggested that the rescinding act might be invalid merely because it offended against "the nature of society and of government," in other words natural law; as Justice Johnson, concurring, put it: "the reason and nature of things: a principle which will impose laws even on the Deity." And in the end Marshall said: "The state of Georgia was restrained, *either* by general principles, which are common to our free institutions, or by the particular provisions of the Constitution of the United States" from passing the rescinding law and applying it to innocent purchasers. (Italics added.) This statement scrambled the various possible arguments in a single indiscriminate mixture.

Yet the importance of the results accomplished by this seemingly turgid rhetoric was considerable. To begin with, it laid the basis for the momentous rule that the state is bound by its own contractual obligations. Marshall may have been toying with the idea of claiming for the Court the power to overthrow laws which violated such agreements on the basis of natural law or "right reason" without reference to any specific constitutional clause. This idea was abroad in the land at the time, and hints of it keep turning up in Supreme Court opinions for many years to come. At first glance it might seem that this carte blanche for judicial governance would be very appealing to Marshall, for it would supply him with a roving commission to invalidate any law he disapproved, subject only to the proviso that the incantations of the natural-law tradition must be recited. But he surely realized that the Court's future lay with the tangible Constitution itself rather than its invisible and most disputable higher-law background, that a Court which claimed the power to go beyond the Constitution would be dispensing with its most valuable support and might end by possessing no power at all. In the long run, therefore, he preferred to moor his arguments in the language of the Constitution. For the moment, however, since the contract clause alone was not yet strong enough to support the great principle that the state must abide by its agreements, he was willing to use the natural law as a supplementary prop. Later, when the contract clause had reached a higher stage of legal maturity, the talk of natural law and right reason was dispensed with and the principle rested squarely and explicitly on the contract clause.

But in the second place and in some ways more important, *Fletcher* v. *Peck* is the first clear precedent for the general proposition that the Supreme Court is empowered to hold state laws unconstitutional. That this power exists is the unstated premise of the whole decision, unstated because Marshall simply assumed that there was no room for argument on the point. He declared what no one would dispute:

> But Georgia cannot be viewed as a single, unconnected sovereign power, on whose legislature no other restrictions are imposed than may be found in its own constitution. She is a part of a large empire; she is a member of the American Union; and that Union has a constitution the supremacy of which all acknowledge, and which imposes limits to the legislatures of the several states, which none claim a right to pass.

Then he blandly took a long leap from this resounding truism to the holding that the Georgia law was invalid. We have seen with what circumspection the Court had been edging toward this climactic declaration in the preceding two decades; now at length its careful efforts were rewarded. The justification for Marshall's assumption of power is to be found by looking to the past, back to the judicial arguments in such cases as *Hayburn* and *Marbury*, back to the acceptance of jurisdiction in *Chisholm*, back to the whole elaborate process by which Marshall and his predecessors built support for the doctrines of judicial independence and judicial review. The argument need not be stated now because that process has imbedded it in the ideology of the nation.

Fletcher v. *Peck*, then, marks the end of the beginning of the

The Establishment of the Right To Decide

Court's long struggle to find its place in the American governmental system. It is a milestone at which we can pause to assess the accomplishments and lessons of the past, and the problems of the future. Some of the initial uncertainties that confronted the four judges in Philadelphia in 1790 have been at least tentatively resolved. The idea of judicial independence has become an operative doctrine. The power of judicial review over national and state legislation has been not only claimed in theory but applied to concrete cases. The judges have begun to learn the arts of judicial governance: the necessity to avoid, if possible, head-on collisions with the dominant political forces of the moment; the undesirability of claiming too much too soon; the great advantage of taking the long view, especially when others take the short; the usefulness of diverting criticism from weakness to strength; the importance of identifying judicial claims to authority with the claims of the Constitution. These doctrines, these arts, are now available to the judiciary as it turns its attention to the cause of national union, and they are potentially of great service to that cause. But we must not mistake half a loaf for the whole; though the preliminaries are over, much remains undone. Judicial independence is a formidable reality, but it remains to be seen whether it can be sustained in the face of real adversity. Judicial review in Marshall's carefully phrased formulation is fairly well accepted, but judicial sovereignty is not; and until the Court's opinion on constitutionality even in debatable cases is regarded as final, the influence of the judiciary on national affairs can only be peripheral. These remaining problems dominate the agenda of the Court's next twenty-five years; and their resolution depends partly on the roll of the historical dice and partly on the wisdom of the judges in directing the institution that has fallen to their charge.

III

The Marshall Court and the Shaping
of the Nation: 1810-1835

So far the story of the Supreme Court has been largely prelude. The judges have been deviled by uncertainties about their own status in the young American polity and about the power and malevolence of the forces that might imperil that status. Since the constitutional agreement of 1789 was inexplicit about the nature and scope of judicial authority, the Court has inherited the responsibility for drawing up its own commission, one line at a time, and the task has been delicate. Only gradually has it become apparent that the Court is being accepted as a symbol of constitutionalism and can therefore count on a solid measure of public support. Only with experience has it become clear to Marshall and his judicial brethren that the Republicans are not after all savage revolutionaries, that their bark is worse than their bite, and that the rule of law can therefore survive even though the Federalist party may not. In such a prelude, amid such uncertainties, the Court has been able to lay the argumentative

54

bases for future accomplishments; it has fashioned some of the tools which may later be used to help govern America. But it has not yet been in a position to exert much real influence on the course of affairs. It has built its own fences with some cunning, but has not so far done much to build the nation.

However, with the War of 1812 and its immediate aftermath a new stage in the Court's history was inaugurated. We have seen that the slow accretion of precedents and confidence culminated in 1810, when the judges at last felt secure enough to hold a state law unconstitutional. Logically, the Court was then ready to begin to make its weight felt in the political order, to defend and foster in a concrete way the principle of national union. Now this logical development was stimulated and strengthened by the war's impact on American attitudes and political alignments.

Many of the old Federalists, especially in New England, had fiercely opposed "Mr. Madison's war," had talked darkly of seceding from the Union, and had espoused a states' rights position strangely reminiscent of the extreme Republicanism of the Virginia and Kentucky resolutions. The politically dominant Republicans, on the other hand, were forced, in defending their war, to embrace the idea of nationalism, and to abjure in part their own localist tradition. Since they were in the ascendancy, this meant that the creed of nationalism enjoyed an unprecedented, if temporary, popularity and—the other side of the coin—that localism was for the moment bereft of really powerful defenders. To be sure localist sentiment soon revived and its exponents were as vocal as ever. But the nationalist spirit, once awakened, could not be dismissed at will. These events had intruded a cross-current in the Republican ideology; leaders like Madison and Monroe though by no means unqualified nationalists were not consistent localists either; the tradition they spoke for was now ambivalent on the great question of the nature of the Union.

This ambivalence persisted for some years and gave John Marshall his opportunity to use the judicial instruments he had been preparing. But his way, though now passable, was still far from easy. The Court after all was in the process of attaining a position more exalted than any attained by a judicial tribunal in modern world history; great tasks were impending. For one thing it was necessary both to confirm and to extend the Court's claim to authority, to transmute "judicial review" into "judicial sovereignty." Granted that it was proper for the Court to adjudge questions of constitutionality, did this imply that the Court's judgment was final? Did it imply that the judges could call the other branches to account even when the question of constitutionality was doubtful? Did it imply that the Court would exercise a general supervision over some governmental affairs that fell outside the traditional judicial orbit?

To Marshall it implied all this, for he was firmly convinced that the more America was guided by judges the happier and more just its system would be. But others, in politics and out, were not ready to bear the Chief Justice's mild yoke, and there was always a threat that overweening judicial power would encounter resistance or counterattack more formidable than its recently established independence could withstand. Though moving onward and upward, then, the Court must still tread carefully.

Secondly and simultaneously, the Court of Marshall's remaining years was engaged in using its still nascent authority to establish the substantive constitutional principles on which the American polity should rest. It was interpreting the document of 1789 so as to provide maximum protection to property rights and maximum support for the idea of nationalism. Usually these two objectives were conjoined, so that a pro-nationalist constitutional doctrine best served the cause of property rights and vice versa. The national government was not at this time much inclined to interfere in commercial affairs, whereas the states, one or the other, presented a constant threat to the stability of currency, the sanctity of debts, or the freedom of business enterprise. Thus Marshall, happily for his peace of mind, was able to assure himself that he made property rights more secure when he deprived the states of power by enhancing the power of the nation. If these two primary values of his had conflicted, his soul-search would have been agonizing. But they seldom did conflict, and his historic achievements in the cause of union were therefore not clouded by confusion of motives.

He had troubles enough without adding internal uncertainty to them. The antinationalist front of the Republicans (soon to be called Democrats) had indeed been impaired, but specific and bitter centers of opposition still developed when specific provocations aroused them, and almost every major decision was met by a storm of intemperate denunciation from some politically potent quarter. Even worse, as the 1820's neared their end, it became increasingly apparent that the tide of states' rights sentiment was rising if not in volume at any rate in intensity. From time to time he was compellingly reminded of a fact that all Supreme Court justices must learn to live with: that the Court's decrees are backed only by its own prestige and ultimately by the willingness of the President to help enforce them. Over and over he was reminded that Congress could destroy in a day the judicial independence that had been building for decades.

In this context Marshall faced his great task of augmenting

the judicial power and shaping the Constitution into a charter for nationalism. These two interwoven themes run through nearly all his decisions; each case raises the question of the Court's authority together with that of nation-state relationship, and the Court must always decide one question in the light of the other, taking care that its nationalist zeal does not compromise its own status or that claims for judicial power are never so extreme as to vitiate the crusade for nationalism. And little by little, in spite of the delicacy of this balancing feat, in spite of the deep antagonism of affected litigants, in spite of the rising wave of states' rights sentiment, the job is done. The Court's empire of decision is extended and stabilized as firmly as it ever can be in a governmental arrangement that rests on inference and acquiescence rather than on final definition. The great operative phrases of the Constitution—the supremacy clause, the contract clause, the necessary and proper clause, the commerce clause—are impregnated with the nationalist meanings so dear to Marshall's heart. And most important of all, these judicially contrived mutations in the character of American constitutionalism are generally accepted by the nation they are designed to guide.

How were these remarkable results achieved? How was the Court able, in the face of these adversities, to have its way? Partly the answer goes back to factors mentioned in previous chapters—the American attachment to the idea of fundamental law and the gradual identification of the Supreme Court with that idea. Partly the answer is to be found in the judges themselves and most of all of course in Marshall—the judicial sense of strategy and timing, the rhetorical virtuosity which should never be undervalued, the capacity to engender respect even among those who disagreed. Partly, as has been said, the difficulties were eased by the temporary ambivalence of Republican opinion on the nature of the Union.

But the Court's progress was also aided by a basic disability of the localist movement—its very lack of unity. The states were so individualistic that they defeated themselves, for it was (and is) a peculiarity of the states' rights doctrine that its partisans were devoted to it only when their own oxen were being gored, when nationalism presented a specific threat to a concrete interest. If states' rights could be associated with a common and long-term economic issue like slavery or the tariff, then the affected states would stand long and firm against their mutual adversary. But if Virginia had a problem today that Maryland did not share, Virginia's outraged protest in the name of states' rights would attract little support from Maryland any more than Maryland's similar protest tomorrow would bring Virginia rushing to her standard. Both states were being true to the fractional principle that lay at the heart of the states' rights doctrine. But, because of their adherence to that principle, the Supreme Court, with its eye steadily on a single target, was spared the calamity of confronting a united opposition. The Court left such potentially unifying issues as the tariff and slavery pretty much alone, and it was not even necessary, then, to divide to conquer, for the opposition had thoughtfully divided itself.

THE COURT OVER THE STATES

One of the Court's great problems was presented either by direct or by implied challenge in nearly every significant case of the era: the problem of its right to review decisions of state courts involving the validity of acts undertaken by the state governments. Such a right was granted to the Court under Section 25 of the Judiciary Act of 1789; state court decisions that denied a claim made in the name of the federal Constitution, laws, or treaties could be reviewed by the Supreme Court by a "writ of error." And of course if the state court was thought to have erred, its judgment could be reversed and any state law it rested on invalidated.

That was the Supreme Court's nominal statutory authority, but it was one thing for Congress to pass such an empowering act and another thing to persuade the states to yield to it. From the first, localists had contended that Section 25 involved an unconstitutional encroachment on state sovereignty, and although the Court had several times exercised this supposedly unwarranted power with comparative impunity, the rumbles of protest had never quite been stilled. The case of *Martin* v. *Hunter's Lessee* in 1816 compelled the Court, which had so far tried to ignore the arguments against Section 25, finally to meet them head on.

The case involved the title to some 300,000 acres of Virginia land which had once belonged to Lord Fairfax but which had been confiscated by the state in Revolutionary times partly on the ground that Fairfax and his heirs were enemy aliens. Virginia had proceeded to grant a section of the land, which it now claimed as its own, to David Hunter, who later sought in the courts of Virginia to eject the Fairfax heirs. But in the meantime of course the Revolution had ended, the Treaty of Peace with Great Britain had been signed, the national Constitution had come into being, and the new national government had been endowed with the power to make treaties. It was argued that both the Treaty of Peace and Jay's Treaty of 1795 confirmed the titles of British subjects to land in America and that the Fairfax title was therefore still valid.

The Marshall Court

In spite of this, the Virginia Court of Appeals held against the Fairfax heirs, and the Supreme Court of the United States, having granted review of this holding on a writ of error, ordered it reversed. The Virginia court, which was headed by Spencer Roane, an ardent states' righter and bitter foe of Marshall, pondered this order for a while and then decided to ignore it, arguing that Section 25 was itself unconstitutional. The Virginia judges conceded of course that they were bound to observe the federal Constitution, but they insisted that the meaning of the Constitution was for them to decide and that the Supreme Court had no power to impose its own interpretation upon them. It was this contention, so fatal to the prospects for both judicial supervision and centralism, that faced the Court in *Martin* v. *Hunter's Lessee*. If the Constitution was to mean whatever the various states wanted it to mean, the cause of national union was lost at the outset.

Justice Story spoke for the Court, Marshall having disqualified himself because he had been financially involved with the Fairfax interests. Story had been appointed by Madison in 1811 as a New England Republican, but now, after five years on the Court, he was as nationalistic in his views as Marshall himself. Indeed the supreme bench consisted of two Federalists and five nominal Republicans, and yet Marshall was seldom to have much difficulty enlisting his fellows in the nationalist crusade. His success in doing so has often been attributed to the witchcraft of his strong and charming personality; Jefferson had once predicted that "it will be difficult to find a character with firmness enough to preserve his independence on the same bench with Marshall." There can be no doubt that Marshall was an immensely attractive and convincing colleague, but it seems reasonable to suppose that the judges who came to share his nationalist views were beguiled not only by him but by a growing awareness that the Court's status and their own depended on the strength of the Union. It is hardly surprising that the Supreme Court, an instrinsically national institution, should be drawn to the doctrine of nationalism.

Story's powerful opinion in this case followed a pattern which can be traced through most of the great nationalistic decisions of the era. In the first place, he felt called upon to argue, or rather to assert, that the Constitution was the creation of "the people of the United States" as the Preamble says, and not of the several states. This contention, which may seem merely abstract, was essential to his purpose. Since at least 1776, most Americans had conceded that the people were the ultimate source of sovereignty and that the people could therefore, as Story says, "invest the general government with all powers which they might deem proper and necessary." If the Constitution was the work of the people, the powers it granted the national government *could* be as extensive as sovereignty itself. But if, on the other hand, the states had created the Constitution, it was arguable that the powers of the national government must stop at the point where they encroached on state sovereignty, and this very argument had been insisted upon by the embattled Virginians. The assertion that the Constitution represented the higher sovereignty of the people enabled Story to controvert the argument that state sovereignty is inviolable; if the people, in enacting the Constitution, wanted to modify state sovereignty, they had an incontestable right to do so.

The second great step in the opinion was to contend that the people *did* want to modify state sovereignty and had given evidence of that desire in the language of the Constitution.

Article III extends the judicial power to all *cases* arising under the Constitution, laws, or treaties. There is no suggestion that the judicial power must stop short if a case originates in a state court rather than a federal. Since the language is general and is not restricted by the context or by necessary implication, it must be assumed that any case presenting a federal question is within reach of the judicial power, whatever may be the tribunal in which it arises.

This opinion contains, in more or less explicit statement, practically all the major items in the bag of tricks the Marshall Court was to use in future years against the minions of disunion. It invokes the doctrine of popular sovereignty to accomplish traditionally Federalist ends, a gambit that was particularly frustrating to the Court's Republican opponents, who were accustomed to think of themselves as the champions of that doctrine. The doctrine is then used by Story to deprecate the idea that state sovereignty was left intact at the time the Union was formed. Next he sets forth the proposition that national powers should be construed generously, a notion disastrous to states' rights when its implications are developed. From these principles "in respect to which no difference of opinion ought to be indulged," as Story says, he is able to infer a supervisory power for the Supreme Court so broad that it embraces all state tribunals. And finally this panoply of authority is used to defend property rights against spoliation by a capricious public. Each of these themes will be echoed over and over in the decisions of the future; each of them serves a vital purpose in the judges' struggle to make America the nation they believed it ought to be.

The specific problem of the *Martin* case—whether the Court's power under Section 25 could be maintained—was not of course entirely settled by Story's argumentative dexterities. In the years that followed, whenever a state felt aggrieved by a Court decision, the familiar cry against Section 25 was again heard. In 1821, in *Cohens* v. *Virginia*, Marshall not only re-iterated Story's basic points but interpreted the Eleventh Amendment, that supposed warranty of states' rights, so as to permit individuals to appeal to the Supreme Court even though a state was the other party in the litigation. The Amendment, said Marshall, prevents individual suits against states only if the action is "commenced" by the individual; if the state has in-itiated the action (for instance, by arresting a person), the per-son can still bring the state into the Supreme Court to defend itself against an appeal.

At this point, the Virginian defenders of states' rights felt that judicial sophistry had surpassed itself, since not even a constitutional amendment had arrested its course. They urged that the Court's authority be curbed by statute or by more carefully drawn amendment, and hereafter throughout the 1820's hardly a session of Congress went by without a proposal to modify, in one way or another, the doctrine of judicial control. These threats were serious enough to alarm the Court and its friends, but in truth none of them ever came very close to succeeding. As John Taylor of Caroline complained, the apathy of the "sister states," when one of their number was assailed, for a long time made a united front of states' rights sentiment impossible to assemble. Meanwhile, decision after decision accustomed the nation to accept the Court's view of its own function; each year that passed, each holding that was sub-mitted to, made it a little harder to question that view. When South Carolina radically assailed the whole principle of nation-alism in the Nullification Ordinance of 1832, its formidable adversaries included not only Andrew Jackson but a federal judiciary which had become a focus of public respect and a symbol of Union.

One handicap of the Supreme Court during these early years and indeed throughout its history was its divorce from the sources of political power. Seven men in Washington, armed with nothing save their robes and their intellects, seem pitiful rivals to state legislatures, congresses, and presidents who command the machinery of government and are backed by the mighty force of the electoral process. But the Court's apparent weakness was also, as we have seen, a kind of opportunity. Because it was an independent, small, cohesive body, it could maintain a long-term view that gave it a decided advantage over opponents divided between a variety of special, temporary concerns and often confused in the basic premises of their opposition.

This advantage is further illustrated by the great Marshallian decisions involving the question of national legislative authority. Story's argument in the *Martin* case that national powers should be liberally construed enabled him to contend that Congress had a right to pass Section 25 and thus to make the Court the dominant tribunal of the nation. But his interest and Marshall's in the doctrine of liberal construction went far beyond its use to bolster judicial status. They wanted to enhance national power in all respects, partly because this would simultaneously restrict the power of the states, but partly too because they anticipated awesome tasks for the nation and wanted to insure that it was constitutionally equipped to deal with them. And

The American Supreme Court

the Court's success in accomplishing this aim must be attributed in no small degree to self-contradiction among the forces that opposed it.

McCulloch v. *Maryland* in 1821 is by almost any reckoning the greatest decision John Marshall ever handed down—the one most important to the future of America, most influential in the Court's own doctrinal history, and most revealing of Marshall's unique talent for stately argument. It involved a state tax on note issues of the Bank of the United States, which had been incorporated by act of Congress in 1816. The government argued that such a tax on a federal instrumentality was invalid and need not be paid. The state replied that the incorporation of the Bank exceeded Congress' constitutional powers and that in any event the states could tax as they willed within their own borders. These contentions raised vast and difficult questions both for the present and the future. The Bank was viewed with special loathing by the states' rights advocates; any decision upholding its claim to exist and denying the state's claim to tax could be counted on to infuriate them. And not the least of their heated objections would be the familiar one that the Court had no power in spite of Section 25 to entertain the cause. On the other hand, it was clear to Marshall, as it has been to posterity, that a national government restricted in its powers by Maryland's narrow interpretation would be incapable of the great tasks that might lie before it.

Speaking for a unanimous Court, Marshall therefore upheld the constitutionality of the Bank's incorporation, and in doing so set down the classic statement of the doctrine of national authority. The argument he advanced was not new; its main outlines had been endlessly debated since the first Congress and Hamilton's famous paper urging the Bank's establishment; and much of it had been given judicial expression by Story in 1816. But Marshall deserves the credit for stamping it with the die of his memorable rhetoric and converting it from a political theory into the master doctrine of American constitutional law.

Because the argument is logical it lends itself to summary, falling into three major phases. The first is concerned with the problem of the nature of the Constitution itself. Two crucial premises are laid down: First, the Constitution emanates from the hand of the sovereign people and speaks in broad language so that it can "be adapted to the various crises of human affairs." We must never forget that "it is a *constitution* we are expounding." These premises infuse the second phase, which concerns the nature of the national government the Constitution created. The people made that government supreme over all rivals within the sphere of its powers (Art. VI), and those powers must be construed generously if they are to be sufficient for the "various crises" of the ages to come.

The third phase is simply the application of these weighty principles. The power to incorporate the Bank is upheld under the clause endowing Congress with the power to make all laws "necessary and proper" for carrying into execution the other powers (Art. I, sec. 8); the words "necessary and proper" are interpreted generously, in accord with the principles advanced, to mean "appropriate" and "plainly adapted." The Maryland tax is invalidated, because since "the power to tax involves the power to destroy," to uphold the tax would grant the state the power to defeat the national government's supremacy; an inferior (in these matters) would be empowered to destroy a superior. But no summary can convey the air of high seriousness that pervades the opinion, the magisterial dignity with which it marches to its conclusions, the sense of righteous certitude with which it announces them. It was such qualities as these that made it persuasive to contemporaries and to the generations to come; and to appreciate these qualities the reader must go to the opinion itself.

The reaction was what might have been expected. In the North and the East the decision was praised; in the South and West, where the Bank was especially unpopular, the Court was roundly condemned. But even in Virginia, the fastness of such philosophers of Republicanism as Jefferson, Roane, and Taylor, the assailants curiously compromised their own position by putting the immediate issue of the Bank ahead of the broader issue of principle. Most of them denounced the Court for *not* holding the incorporation statute unconstitutional, thus of course tacitly conceding that the Court had the power to do so. Yet surely if the Court had the exalted power of overthrowing an act of Congress, it was not unreasonable to suppose that it also had the right to disapprove state laws. And if it did have these high prerogatives the Court must have some discretion in exercising them, that is, it could not be condemned merely because Spencer Roane, wielding the same power, would have decided the case differently.

In short most of the critics conceded too much for the good of their own criticisms. Their proper course would have been to deny that the Court had any business judging the validity of either national or state laws. But as usual they were more concerned about the immediate, concrete issue than they were about such a general doctrine as judicial sovereignty or even states' rights; and once again the Court profited from the fact that it alone seemed to understand the value of consistency and generality.

Much the same lesson can be drawn from the "Steamboat

Monopoly Case," *Gibbons* v. *Ogden* in 1824, in which the Court was confronted for the first time by the problem of interpreting the commerce clause. A quarter-century before, the New York legislature had granted Robert R. Livingston and Robert Fulton the exclusive right to steamboat navigation in the waters of New York, and in the course of time the monopoly had extracted a similar privilege from Louisiana. The value of this controlling position in the two great port states of the nation was of course enormous, and rival states were deeply resentful of the arrangement. The *Gibbons* case involved an action for encroachment on the monopoly, and the defendant contended that the state had no right to grant it in the first place, because navigation is "commerce among the several states," which is the business of Congress.

This contention raised a series of questions that were destined for long and checkered careers in the development of constitutional law. First, what *is* interstate commerce? Does the term cover only buying and selling, or does it apply to such activities as navigation? Second, once we have determined what interstate commerce is, what is the extent of the power to regulate it? Third, what is the effect on the states of this grant of power to Congress? Must they stay out of the field altogether, or do they have a concurrent right to control it? It is not too much to say that the future of America as a nation depended on the answers that were given to these questions.

And Marshall, with his usual foresight, was well aware that he stood at another major constitutional crossroad. The opinion, like so many of his great ones, is a deft blend of boldness and restraint. In answer to the first two questions, he advanced the kind of broad, nationalistic definitions that the Hamiltonian tradition approved. Commerce, he said, is not merely buying and selling; it includes "every species of commercial inter-course," and this is true whether we are talking of either inter-state or foreign commerce. Nor does interstate commerce stop at state boundaries; a journey that begins in Boston and ends in Philadelphia is subject to congressional power from start to finish. Of course, so inclusive a definition amply covers naviga-tion. As for the extent of Congress' power to regulate a subject, once it is found to be in interstate commerce, that power is "complete in itself, may be exercised to its utmost extent, and acknowledges no limitations other than are prescribed in the Constitution." It is no less than the power "to prescribe the rule by which commerce is to be governed."

Perhaps only in the perspective of the future can it be under-stood how much these words meant; a twentieth-century ob-server looking back on them is impressed because he knows that the definitions have proved elastic enough to justify all the extensive commercial enterprises in which the national government has since engaged. But to contemporaries the most urgent question was yet to come: are the states precluded from acting in the commercial area thus defined? And at this point Marshall grew curiously evasive. He stated sympathetically the argument that the commerce power is exclusive, remarked that it had "great force" and said: ". . . the court is not satisfied that it has been refuted." He came as close to formally approv-ing the doctrine as he could without quite doing so. But, he went on, it is not now necessary to decide this issue, because the New York monopoly law conflicts with a federal coasting license statute. Whether or not the commerce clause alone would invalidate the state law, surely it must be admitted that the federal coasting license law does, for the Constitution makes congressional enactments "the supreme law of the land." The lucrative but controversial monopoly was thus at last brought to an end.

Once again, as so often in the past, Marshall had managed to achieve imperishable results while side-stepping the area of greatest controversy. In other commerce clause cases he refined the notion of interstate (and foreign) commerce somewhat further by holding that goods were still subject to national control so long as they remained in their original shipping packages (the "original package doctrine"); and confused the question of state regulatory power still more by allowing a state to maintain a dam that blocked a navigable stream. No watchful guardian of states' rights could contend that Marshall had erected constitutional barriers to all state commercial regulation. Surely he had implied that some such regulation might be prohibited by the commerce clause alone, and surely his dicta about the extent of the commerce power had opened up the possibility of prodigious congressional regulation in this field. But it was present actualities, not implications and possibilities, that most concerned his contemporaries, and they found it hard to condemn a judicial stroke that slew the hated monopoly, whatever the flourishes that accompanied it. Jefferson and a few like him were horrified by *Gibbons*, but in general the decision was welcomed; the fact that it did after all overthrow a state law and hammer a few more nails in the coffin of state sovereignty was easy to minimize in the face of its immediately popular conclusion.

JUDICIAL ALLIES AND PRIVATE RIGHTS

One of the Supreme Court's peculiar characteristics is that it attempts to decide questions of policy without the advantage of conventional political resources. The judges have no organized party machine to call on for guidance and encouragement; they are spared both the penalties and the benefits of direct electoral support. But this does not mean of course that the Court has no constituency, if we can use that word in a somewhat looser and more informal sense than is usual. No institution in a democratic society could become and remain potent unless it could count on a solid block of public opinion that would rally to its side in a pinch. And the Supreme Court has historically been blessed with two kinds of supporters—those who venerate it and are prepared to defend it as the symbol of continuity and fairness, who are attached to the idea of the rule of law; and those who happen to be gratified by the course of policy the judges are pursuing at the moment. In practice the latter invariably claim also to be the former, and perhaps the problem of separately identifying the two groups is futile and somewhat academic. It is enough for our purposes to say that the Marshall Court had such a constituency to draw on and that the growth of constitutional doctrine on the subject of private rights is illuminated if we realize that this is so.

An essential element in that constituency, though by no means the whole of it, was the American legal fraternity, or as it has been called in a fine phrase, "the inner republic of bench and bar." In these early days lawyers were already occupying the pivotal position in American political affairs that they have occupied ever since. And they tended to reinforce the Supreme Court, partly no doubt because they represented the affluent "haves" who would profit from the stable, nationalized structure Marshall was building, but partly too because their training had taught them to esteem the rule of law which Marshall and his associates stood for. It was not only that men like Wil-

liam Pinckney and Daniel Webster vindicated Marshallian doctrine with the magic of their oratory in formal argument before
the supreme bench; they and their lesser colleagues also helped,
in letters, in conversations, in appearances before lower courts,
in state legislatures, and in Congress, to generate the atmosphere
of consent that made Marshall's achievements possible.

These stout allies played a significant part during Marshall's
era in the development and acceptance of doctrines protecting
the property owner, most particularly by way of the contract
clause of the Constitution. In fact if their activities were not part
of the historical record, they would have to be postulated in
order to account for a process of legal growth that would otherwise seem autonomous. It will be remembered that Marshall
had stepped very tentatively in *Fletcher* v. *Peck*, the first contract clause decision. The principle that the state must abide
by its own contractual commitments rested on flimsy historical
grounds and presented certain grave logical difficulties; therefore the vague mandates of natural law were invoked to augment
the force of the contract clause argument. Two years later, in
1812, he offered an interpretation of *Fletcher* that made it sound
less ambiguous than it was: in that case, he said, it was decided
"on solemn argument and much deliberation" that the contract
clause "extends to contracts to which a State is a party." The
statement of the point is clear enough at this stage, but it is
after all only a statement; nothing apparent had happened to
quiet the misgivings he seemed to have in *Fletcher* about the
doctrine's acceptability.

Seven years later the famous case *Dartmouth College* v.
Woodward came to the Supreme Court. The question was
whether the state legislature could validly alter the charter
which had been granted to Dartmouth College in 1769 by the

British crown. A complex imbroglio of theology and politics had resulted in a law changing the name of the college to Dartmouth University and vesting control over it in trustees and overseers largely appointed by the governor; in effect, Dartmouth was to be converted into a public institution. The old trustees fought back by pointing out that the charter had granted them the sole right to fill vacancies in their number "forever" and contending among other things that the state law violated the federal contract clause. This was a bold assertion and seemingly not a very promising one, since it involved, in addition to the heretofore somewhat doubtful idea that the state is bound by its own contracts, two even more novel propositions: that a charter is such a contract and that it is inviolable even though its holders have no "beneficial interest" at stake.

It might be thought that the burden of all these meanings would be more than the contract clause could bear, especially when we consider that Marshall himself appeared to have so little confidence in it only nine years earlier. But Marshall not only affirmed all three interpretations but did so with an economy of argument unusual for him. On the first he offered no argument at all, simply taking it for granted that the state must stick to its agreements; the trimmings drawn from the natural law tradition were now dispensed with, and the contract clause alone was the basis for decision. The idea that a corporate charter is a contract within the meaning of the clause was also assumed rather than argued. Finally he came to the only point that really troubled him—that the contract clause was primarily designed to protect the private property rights of individuals and that the trustees have no such beneficial interest in Dartmouth College; they would not personally lose anything if the charter were overthrown. But, said Marshall, although the framers of the contract clause may have been chiefly concerned with protecting private property, they did not use language that excludes a charitable institution like Dartmouth, and we must therefore assume it is included. "The case, being within the words of the rule, must be within its operation likewise" unless the result would be "obviously absurd, or mischievous, or repugnant to the general spirit" of the Constitution.

The startling thing about the *Dartmouth College* case is not this last point, which follows reasonably enough if we accept the two that precede it, nor yet those two points themselves; but the fact that they were announced so confidently and seem to have provoked so little dissent. Indeed the Superior Court of New Hampshire, though holding against the trustees, had conceded that the contract clause extended to contracts between states and individuals and had assumed that a charter granting privileges to individuals for their own benefit would be protected by the contract clause. Yet by these concessions the contract clause, once apparently innocuous, became a mighty instrument for the judicial protection of property rights against state abridgment. How did it happen that Marshall could forge such an instrument so off-handedly? How did the tentative suggestion of *Fletcher* in 1810 become the confident assertion of *Dartmouth* in 1819?

The explanation is that the Court's "constituency" had been at work on its behalf in the meantime. The idea that the contract clause might serve to protect private property from the states and the corollary idea that corporate charters could be included in such protection—these embryonic ideas had caught hold in the minds of lawyers and judges, had been fostered and developed by them, and had thereby been raised to the status of mature constitutional doctrines. By 1819, they were so well intrenched that the Supreme Court needed to do little more than stamp them with its formal sanctions. The *Dartmouth* decision is important then, not for its own accomplishments but for its acknowledgment of results already achieved. Businessmen, secure in the possession of inviolable state-granted charters, could thank their stars for "the inner republic of bench and bar" as well as for John Marshall.

Marshall wanted in fact to improve the property holders' lot even further. In the same year he invalidated a New York bankruptcy law on the ground that it infringed the contract clause. The special vice of this law was that it released debtors from obligations contracted before its passage. A creditor might legitimately feel aggrieved if he loaned money under one set of rules and was forced to try to collect it under another. But, it was argued, if the law already exists, the lender knowingly takes the risk that his debtor will be released by bankruptcy and therefore cannot complain of unfairness if it so turns out. However, Marshall, in holding that the Constitution barred retrospective interference with contracts, used language intimating that *prospective* interferences were also prohibited. His ambitious objective was to forbid any state law that impaired contracts in any way, and the acceptance of such a principle would have greatly enhanced the value of the contract clause as an instrument for the protection of private rights. But at this point even his usually acquiescent brethren called a halt, and in 1827 the Court voted, four to three, to uphold a state bankruptcy law as applied to debts contracted after its passage. Marshall dissented, and it is plain that the decision bitterly disappointed him; but he had much reason for self-congratulation all the same. With the help of the contemporary bench and bar, he

had transmuted a clause of modest pretensions into a broad in-
hibition on the commercial laws of the states. He had maneu-
vered America a few steps closer to his own idea of the good
society.

THE ACHIEVEMENT OF JOHN MARSHALL

Few intellectual feats are more difficult than the assessment of
history while we are living it, and perhaps the problem is all
the greater for those who are themselves playing the leading
roles. In his last years, Marshall was beset with misgivings about
America's future, full of gloomy convictions that he had failed
in his campaign to establish judicial sovereignty and to cement
the bonds of national union. The states' rights movement was
waxing ever stronger and more vocal under the ministrations of
John C. Calhoun; the Court had recently been defied in two
spectacular cases by Georgia, and President Jackson's unwillingness to back the judges had underlined the Court's ultimate de-
pendency on external support. The old Federalist dream of
rule by "the wise, the rich, and the good" seemed more chimeri-
cal than ever, as the spirit of Jacksonian democracy swept the
nation.

But, ominous though these developments appeared, Marshall
was wrong to think that they spelled the failure of his programs.
Not even he, the architect-in-chief, realized how securely the
cornerstones of American constitutionalism had been laid. His
error probably was that he hoped for absolute certitude in a
system that had been dedicated by its framers to the principle
of relativism. We cannot say that the doctrine of judicial sovereignty was established beyond the shadow of doubt by *Cohens*

v. *Virginia* in 1821, or that the broad construction of national powers was settled once and for all by *McCulloch* v. *Maryland* and *Gibbons* v. *Ogden*, or that the *Dartmouth* case stilled all uncertainties about the contract clause. We cannot say that at one moment the constitutional basis for union was an aspiration and at the next a firm reality, for constitutional history does not move in this way. The vagueness of the Constitution on these issues gave the Court its chance to be creative, but by the same token it was decreed that the creations would never be final and perfect. The Court's title to power, being inferred rather than explicitly stated, must always be somewhat tentative; interpretations of the Constitution, being fashioned by the historical context rather than by the fiat of 1789, must submit to the verdict of later history, as well as the past. With all his subtlety and shrewdness, Marshall's mind was attracted by absolutes, and the contingency of the constitutional universe never ceased to trouble him.

But if we can tolerate, as Marshall could not, a world of half-certainty (and if we enjoy, as he did not, the perspective of the future), we can see that his forebodings were excessive, and his accomplishments greater than he knew. The doctrine of judicial sovereignty was still subject to occasional challenge in moments of stress; men like Jackson and Calhoun were unwilling to admit that the Supreme Court was the *only* authority on the Constitution's meaning. But surely the judicial monopoly, though imperfect, was very impressive. The nation in general thought of the Court as the principal authority and conceded its right to supervise the states in most matters. When the Court impinged on the great primary interests of a state or region, a line might be drawn; but in the considerable distance before that line was reached judicial sovereignty held its sway. The Supreme Court was now far more serene and formidable than the precariously balanced institution Marshall had taken over in 1801. America's devotion to the idea of fundamental law and the Court's ability to capitalize on opponents' errors had made sure of that.

This establishment of judicial hegemony was itself a highly important victory in the struggle to promote the principle of national union, for it meant (with the qualifications already mentioned) that the Constitution spoke with one voice throughout America. But the other substantive principles Marshall had laid down also served that purpose and were also more solidly fixed than Marshall, in his somber old age, imagined. The national-power doctrines of *McCulloch* and *Gibbons* were to have their great day in a more remote future when the national government felt inclined to use the constitutional sinews Marshall's court had provided; until then their significance was more moral than practical. But the corollary doctrine—that the states may not encroach on these federally reserved realms—was well accepted and immediately relevant. These limitations on state power based on the doctrine of national supremacy, plus such specific limitations as those derived from the contract clause, helped open the way to the development of commercial enterprise on a national scale in the next half-century.

Marshall was right in thinking that he had failed to resolve for America the great problem of nation-state relationships. No court could finally settle an issue of such dimensions, an issue that had already brought the nation near the brink of civil war. But he might justifiably have felt that he and his Court had made a priceless contribution to its settlement, had fashioned out of judicial materials an ideology of seasoned strength to which those who cared for the Union could repair, had established a pattern of control that would help to shore up the Union even though nothing but bloodshed could ultimately save it. He could have comforted himself with the thought that no court in world history had ever done so much to affect the destiny of a great nation.

IV

The Court under Taney: The Natural History of Judicial Prestige

When John Marshall died in 1835, the anguish of his admirers was compounded partly of grief for a beloved national figure and partly of apprehension that Jackson would appoint Roger B. Taney to succeed him. It is one of the commonplaces of American history that those who have learned to live with the governmental order of their own day nurse an often excessive dread of its passing. They forget how many times their forebodings of the past have turned out to be bugbears; they forget that the bonds of continuity in America are remarkably strong. And so it was in 1835. Taney had been a staunch opponent of the Bank of the United States and had, as Secretary of the Treasury, deprived the Bank of the federal deposits that were its lifeblood. This made him, in the eyes of anti-Jacksonians, a "political hack" and "a supple, cringing tool of power," for the Bank was their darling. The prospect of a Court appointed by Democratic presidents and headed by Taney seemed dark indeed; Marshall's carefully wrought jurisprudence would be demolished and the nation would be exposed to the unchecked ravages of agrarian, states' rights radicalism.

Their depression deepened when the event they had feared actually occurred. Taney was appointed, and confirmed by the Senate after a bitter wrangle in March of 1836; five members of the Court were now Jackson appointees, only Story and Thompson surviving from the Marshallian golden age. Webster, the "godlike Daniel" whose name and heart were so intimately associated with the old Court, wrote: "Judge Story thinks the Supreme Court is *gone,* and I think so too." Then three decisions handed down in Taney's first term seemed to confirm their misgivings. Each of the cases had been heard by Marshall, but decision had been postponed; the holdings of the new Taney Court were in each case at variance with the position Marshall would have taken, according to his close friend Justice Story. The dismay of the Whigs was acute. "Under the progressive genius of this new judicial administration," said one journal, "we can see the whole fair system of the Constitution beginning to dissolve like the baseless fabric of a vision."

For a long time historians accepted these despairing outbursts as if they actually, or at any rate nearly, described the constitutional policies of the Taney Court. The legend of Taney and his brethren as radical democrats, hostile to property rights, nationalism, and Marshall's memory, was stronger than the facts that would have emerged from a reading of the decisions themselves. But as the decisions finally were read and compared with those of Marshall's time, as the whole doctrinal course of the Taney Court was traced, it became apparent that the legend was badly misleading. The old jurisprudence had not been broken down after all, or even very greatly altered: the claims of property were still well protected, the nation was not constitutionally fragmented, judicial power was not surrendered. In fact, the position of the Supreme Court as the final arbiter of constitutional questions had become, within a few years of Taney's accession, more secure than ever before. The concept of judicial sovereignty, which Marshall had nurtured so lovingly and defended against so many challenges, was by 1840 an almost unquestioned premise of American government.

This congenial result, unexpected by the Webster-Story fraternity and long unnoticed by history, was achieved in perfectly unsurprising ways. The living Marshall himself of course deserves much of the credit. Numerous though his enemies were, even they had found it hard to resist being impressed by his dignity, his self-righteousness, and his intellectual power; and his constitutional edifice had been well made.

But the death of the great Chief Justice was almost as decisive as his life in bringing about the triumph of judicial sovereignty. For one thing it made him a saint. Within a surprisingly short time the justices of the Supreme Court, regardless of who appointed them, were paying almost unanimous lip service to his memory; those who had chided him so willingly while he was alive now cited him, like scripture, in their own behalf and flinched at the charge that he would have disagreed with them. For another thing, Marshall's death diverted judicial partisanship, or rather turned it upside down. Though many Americans came to venerate Marshall, many others could never forget that he was a Federalist and a very opinionated one at that, and thus a residue of animosity always handicapped the Marshall Court.

Now the Chief and a majority of his associates were Jackson-approved, and this meant that the anti-judicial tradition of the Democrats lost much of its edge. On the other hand, the Whigs (the successors to the now-dead Federalist party), though they might bemoan the loss of their idol and deplore the advent of Taney, were committed to a projudicial philosophy they could not lightly forswear. Their natural propensity to support the Court could be depended upon to reassert itself when and if they realized that the Taney regime was not likely to attempt a real constitutional revolution. Unless the Court erred on the side of either extreme—unless it enraged the Democrats by an excess of Marshallian nationalism or antagonized the Whigs by an outright reversion to localism—the chances for a kind of judicial "era of good feelings" were very good.

Whether the chance should become a reality depended of course on the wisdom of the judges who confronted this opportunity. The old idea that they seriously undermined Marshall's constitutional structure has already been mentioned; there is very little to it. But in recent years there has been some disposition to reverse the idea, and to treat the Court of the Taney era as if its doctrines were a consistent extension in all important respects of tendencies Marshall set going, as if no concessions at all to shifting political winds had been made.

The trouble is that neither of these comparatively neat analyses will quite square with the untidy, pragmatic welter of doctrines that has actually been bequeathed to us by the Taney Court. It is true that the jurisdiction of the federal courts was in some ways extended beyond the limits Marshall had recognized —in admiralty cases, for example, and in cases involving the right of corporations to bring federal suits. It is true that the basic dogmas of Marshall's contract-clause interpretation were not challenged and that in some cases the Taney Court was as dogmatic about the sanctity of contracts as even Marshall had been. It is true that the national government's supremacy over the states was repeatedly upheld. But it is also true that the Court elsewhere restricted the range of jurisdiction that is asserted or implied in some of Marshall's great opinions, qualified the constitutional privileges enjoyed by corporations, and granted the states a degree of autonomy in commercial matters that Marshall would undoubtedly have denied them.

The fact is that the Court from 1836 until 1857 was pursuing a non-doctrinaire course to which only the loosest kind of descriptive generalizations can apply. The Court was adjusting itself to the contours of a changing America, relaxing the rigidities of Marshallian dogma when that seemed desirable, retaining or strengthening others, and fashioning some new dogmas of its own, producing a constitutional jurisprudence that had been pragmatically fitted to the nation of the day. If we see the process either in terms of pure judicial imperialism or pure judicial abnegation, we are missing the important point—that the Taney Court by giving ground at some salients was able to advance upon others, thus maintaining a quantum of jurisdiction at least equal to that exercised by Marshall but composed of elements somewhat different from those the great Chief Justice himself might have chosen. And we might miss the even more significant point that the result of this adjustment process was to fortify the judicial power by creating an atmosphere of public acceptance more complete than the Court had ever before enjoyed. Marshall's historic task had been to establish the frontiers of judicial supervision; the function of the Court under Taney was to consolidate the most essential of these gains by a deft combination of tenacity and flexibility. The function was so well performed that not even the monumental indiscretion of the *Dred Scott* decision could quite destroy the judicial imperium.

THE NATION-STATE PROBLEM AND THE COURT'S
POLICY OF MODERATION

The theme of the adjustment process by which this result was achieved was compromise. To be sure, this theme was far from new in the Court's history; even Marshall had been well aware that half a loaf is sometimes better than none, and no wise Court has ever forgotten this platitude. But the need to compromise is a matter of degree depending in part on the historic context. Marshall in the most creative period of his tenure faced a situation that permitted the Court to pursue a comparatively bold and unambiguous policy with impunity. In the years from 1836 to 1857, the American political world was torn by conflicts so bitter that a frankly doctrinaire Court would have wounded both itself and the cause of union. As always, the Court was dedicated to keeping the Union secure, if only because its own existence depended on that security. But there is a season for everything, and in the climate of the Taney era the Court could best sustain the Union by preserving its own status as a national tribunal. And that meant that constitutional doctrines must be framed in a spirit of moderation.

One of the 1837 decisions that so alarmed the Whigs was *Mayor of New York* v. *Miln,* in which the Court had upheld a state regulation applying to ships entering the port of New York. The law impinged on foreign commerce, and Marshall's disciple Story argued that it should be overturned under the doctrine, which he derived from the Steamboat Monopoly Case, that Congress' power over foreign and interstate commerce is exclusive. This was of course the extreme nationalist position applied with a rigor that Marshall himself had not insisted upon. The other extreme was Justice Thompson's view that the states could regulate interstate and foreign commerce as much as they chose unless the state law conflicted with an actual federal statute.

But the Court majority steered between, sustaining the law on the ground that the state had merely been exercising its "police power" for the welfare of its citizens, not regulating commerce; thus the question of whether the national commerce power was exclusive did not arise. A flat answer to that question, either yes or no, would have infuriated an important segment of American opinion. The Court's resort to what has been called the "convenient apologetics" of the police power enabled it to avoid both the frying pan and the fire; and the additional advantage was that the doctrine was arguably rooted in one of Marshall's own decisions which had permitted a state, on similar grounds, to block a navigable stream. Even the Whigs, if they had really thought the matter over, could not reasonably contend that a prolocalist revolution had taken place.

Although the police-power doctrine was therefore in some ways very convenient, the distinction it made was always slippery, for it depended, as Taney was to say, on the idea that a state regulation which affected commerce had been passed with the motive of protecting health and welfare, rather than regulating commercial affairs. Motive is always an elusive entity. Moreover, since Revolutionary times, the states had woven a complex network of regulations which were frankly commercial and which often touched foreign and interstate transactions: here the police-power "apologetics" were not even relevant. So the Court found it increasingly difficult to evade the direct question of whether the states could regulate commerce as such. In 1851, they resolved the question, again by compromise. The states, said the Court, are precluded from regulating commerce as such when the particular subjects regulated are "in their nature national, or admit only of one uniform system . . . of regulation." On the other hand, if the subject is one that is local in character, appropriate for diverse plans of regulation, depending on local peculiarities, the states may regulate that commerce until Congress itself chooses to take over the subject (*Cooley* v. *Board of Wardens*).

This ingenious disengagement from the horns of the dilemma was not entirely satisfying to those, like Taney himself, who had argued for full concurrent state power in the commercial field; nor to those all-out nationalists, like Justice McLean, who had insisted that the states must leave commerce strictly alone. But neither localist nor nationalist could claim that the Court had wholly yielded to the other; each could justifiably feel that the announced doctrine in some part embodied his views.

In other fields a comparably moderate realignment of doctrine can be traced. The other two 1837 decisions that had alarmed the disciples of Marshall like a fire bell in the night were *Charles River Bridge* v. *Warren Bridge Co.* and *Briscoe* v. *Bank of Kentucky*. The first involved an application of the contract clause, that sacred cow of Marshall's jurisprudence, and because the Court refused to find in the clause new restrictions on state power, the cry of heresy was raised.

The proprietors of a toll bridge in Massachusetts argued that their state-granted charter implied a promise that the legislature would not authorize a competing bridge; in short that, without explicitly saying so, the state had endowed them with a constitutionally guaranteed monopoly. The Court simply held that no such inferences would be drawn; public grants should be strictly construed. There is no challenge to the basic principles of Marshall's contract-clause doctrine—that a charter is a contract that binds the state—nor is there evidence in later contract-clause cases that the Taney Court was reckless of property rights, as the Whigs had feared. The states were held to the letter of the doctrines Marshall had enunciated, and the most that can be said is that the new Court usually declined to expand those doctrines so as further to inhibit state powers. By thus conceding the states some leeway in commercial affairs and at the same time insisting that they abide by the promises they had actually made, the Court had once more found a middle—and generally popular—ground.

As for the *Briscoe* case, it undoubtedly represents a concession to localism. One of the evils that had most perturbed men of substance during the Articles of Confederation period was state issuance of currency, and the Founding Fathers had hoped to debar a return to that sorry state of affairs by providing, in Article I, section 10, that no states might "emit bills of credit." Marshall had enforced the clause rigorously when Missouri issued interest-bearing certificates receivable for debts due the state. Since they circulated as money, they were bills of credit. But now Justice McLean, in a Court opinion that is a triumph of incoherency, approved the issuance of currency by a bank owned and controlled by Kentucky. An uninitiated observer might protest that such a bank was the equivalent of the state itself and equally bound by the constitutional prohibition. Justice Story, who dissented, had no doubts about it. But the new Court thought otherwise, and state autonomy in money matters was given increased vitality.

But against the centrifugal thrust of such a decision and a few others of a similar tenor, we can balance a series of judgments which reasserted the principle of national supremacy: for example, a ruling that the incomes of federal employees are exempt from state taxation under the doctrine of *McCulloch* v. *Maryland;* a second that the extradition of fugitives from justice to foreign countries is an exclusive prerogative of the national government; and a third permitting a corporation chartered in one state to do business in another unless specifically barred by the second state's laws. In this last case partisans had argued on the one side that Alabama *could* not, under the "privileges and immunities" clause (Art. IV, sec. 2), exclude a Georgia-chartered corporation, and on the other side that the corporation was *automatically* excluded, without a specific Alabama law, because the Georgia charter was useless anywhere else. Characteristically the Taney Court faced by these extreme contentions chose to compromise.

And compromise was appropriate to the Court's historic circumstances in a double sense. After the burst of creative enterprise under Marshall, the judiciary had need to slow the pace of its constitution-making process so that America could grow used to the house John Marshall had built, so that the doctrines could be adjusted a little to fit the facts of the changing economic order, so that the judicial power could be consolidated. Great advances in history, if they endure, are often followed by such a period of retardation and adaptation. But beyond this, a propitiating temper was called for by the conditions of the day, especially when the great question of nation-state relationships was even indirectly raised. For America was moving toward Armageddon with frightening inexorability, and passions were stirring as never before. If the task of the Marshall Court had been to champion nationalism against the states' rights movement, the task of the Court in Taney's era was to champion temperance and reason against the extremism that threatened to dissever the Republic. For a long time it performed that task remarkably well.

THE PRIDE OF POWER AND THE SLAVERY QUESTION

But throughout these years, as the judges charted point by point their path of moderation, a specter stood near their elbows, and as time passed this presence became harder and harder to ignore. Its name, of course, was slavery. In an attempt to exorcise it, the Court mortally endangered the judicial temple which they and their predecessors had so painfully erected. For a time it seemed that the labor of nearly seventy years would be blown away by the holocaust following one dramatic lapse from judicial self-restraint.

It is easy for a modern observer to see, looking back, that the slavery question was too big and too explosive to be decided by a court. We know, whatever mythologists may say, that there are practical as well as technical limits on the Court's jurisdiction. The great fundamental decisions that determine the course of society must ultimately be made by society itself. If they are also, as they are apt to be, decisions that profoundly engage the emotions of the whole people, this is all the more reason for the judiciary to leave them alone; the Court's place is not on the battlefield or in the center of the political arena. And we know that, as it turned out, only bloodshed could settle the slavery issue.

The judges of the 1850's knew some of these things but unfortunately not all, and others were perhaps too easily forgotten in the heat of the moment. They should have realized that their power was built on a lively sense of its own limitations; this was the lesson of the Court's past successes—and failures. They should have known that slavery was a judicial untouchable, for it had already, in 1850, brought the nation to the brink of civil war. But they were children of their time as well as judges. By the 1850's the slavery issue was clouding the gaze of seemingly wise men all over America; it is perhaps too much to expect that the vision of the Supreme Court would remain unimpaired.

For a while the Court majority resisted the temptation to plunge into the flames. To be sure, as early as 1842 Justice Story had struck back-handedly at slavery when, speaking for the Court, he overturned a Pennsylvania law. It conflicted, he said, with the federal Fugitive Slave Law, and he went on gratuitously to hold that *any* state legislation touching fugitive slaves was invalid because the national power over that subject was exclusive. Since the national law was almost unworkable without state co-operation, the effect of this decision was to hamper the apprehension of fugitive slaves under the guise of defending the power to apprehend them. The decision was angrily criticized. But the tumult such as it was soon died down, and the Court thereafter left the slavery question pretty much to the mercies of the political branches of government.

In 1851, it was confronted with the contention that slaves had become free when they entered free states or territories. Behind this argument lurked the perilous question of whether Congress could prohibit slavery in the territories of the United States, as it had done in the Missouri Compromise. With nice discretion, the judges skirted the volcano's edge, holding in *Strader* v. *Graham* that the status of the Negroes in question depended on the laws of the state where they now lived—Kentucky. Since Kentucky regarded them as slaves, the Supreme Court was bound by that fact; and the question of their status during former sojourns in free areas did not arise.

The Court under Taney

By this kind of circumspection the carefully nurtured judicial prestige was temporarily kept intact in these hazardous hours. But the Court's high repute was in some ways its danger. The political order was abundantly demonstrating its inability to cope with the slavery issue without dissevering the nation. The line defining the practical boundaries of the Court's power, though implicitly recognized in decisions of the past, had seldom been acknowledged, and prevailing mythology tended to obscure its existence. Perhaps, then, this highly esteemed group of nine men could succeed where the political parties were so grievously failing. Perhaps a pronouncement from them would settle the questions evoking the slavery controversy, or at any rate help in settling the thorniest of them all—the question of slavery in the territories. The nation was in deadly jeopardy. It would be tragic for the Court to withhold its hand, if that hand might save the Union.

Such exalted ideas of the Court's power were advanced repeatedly during these years by supposedly responsible statesmen and publicists. The judges were sure to listen, and they were tempted to heed. Perhaps, however, they had also been impressed by the ominous words of Northerners like Seward and Chase, who had accused the Court of partiality to slavery and denied that the country need accept a proslavery decision. The old familiar challenge to judicial sovereignty had not been heard much lately, and its reappearance now may have given the judges pause. At all events a majority of them were still apparently unconvinced that they could bell the cat when *Dred Scott* v. *Sandford* came before them in 1856. Scott had been taken as a slave into Illinois and into the northern part of the Louisiana Purchase. Illinois law forbade slavery, and the Louisiana Purchase territory north of the southern boundary of Missouri had been declared free by the Missouri Compromise in 1820–21. Scott, now in Missouri, sued his present owner in federal court, arguing that these journeys to free areas had made him a free man. This raised the fiery question of whether Congress could bar slavery from the territories, but did not require the Court to answer the question. The judges might have replied, under the analogy of the *Strader* case, that they were bound by Missouri law, regardless of Scott's status when he had lived elsewhere. Since Missouri regarded him as a slave that would settle the matter, and the problem of Congress' power need not be answered, pro or con. A majority of the Supreme Court agreed to take this course; an opinion was actually written by Justice Nelson.

But at least one judge, McLean, was dissatisfied with this prudent arrangement. It became known that he, an ambitious politician and a firm abolitionist, intended to dissent, arguing that Scott became free when he entered the free territory of the Louisiana Purchase. This necessarily involved the contention that Congress had the power to enact the Missouri Compromise which had made that area free. A majority of his fellow judges believed in fact that the Compromise was invalid, and they were unwilling to let McLean go unanswered, if the question was to be posed at all. Besides there was always the beguiling idea that a forthright statement from the Court might settle the whole, terrible issue and retrieve simultaneously the cause of both the Union and the South. Cheered on by his fellows and by the newly elected President James Buchanan, Taney therefore produced the most disastrous opinion the Supreme Court has ever issued. Dred Scott, he said, cannot bring suit in federal courts, first, because Negroes are not and cannot be citizens in the meaning of the federal Constitution; second, because, since the Missouri Compromise exceeded Congress' powers and is unconstitutional, he is still a slave in spite of his sojourn in free territory; and, third, because Missouri law regards him as a slave and the Supreme Court is here bound by Missouri's determination.

Eight separate opinions, including the Chief's, were filed by the judges in this case, and the task of unraveling them is more formidable than it is rewarding. What mattered to the nation was that a six-judge majority had denied the right of Negroes to be citizens and the right of Congress to control slavery in the territories.

The tempest of malediction that burst over the judges seems to have stunned them; far from extinguishing the slavery controversy, they had fanned its flames and had, moreover, deeply endangered the security of the judicial arm of government. No such vilification as this had been heard even in the wrathful days following the Alien and Sedition Acts. Taney's opinion was assailed by the Northern press as a wicked "stump speech" and was shamefully misquoted and distorted. "If the people obey this decision," said one newspaper, "they disobey God." Senator Seward fostered a dramatic but improbable story that Buchanan and Taney had villainously plotted this stroke on behalf of the slavery interests in a whispered tête-à-tête during the President's inauguration ceremonies, and the idea of a corrupt bargain between President, Congress, and Court became a theme of party politics in the next few years.

Of course no such explicit conspiracy existed. But Taney had connived in an exchange of information between Justices Catron and Grier and the incoming President, apparently out of sincere conviction that the leader of the nation in such parlous times should be informed about so grave an issue. It was not the least of his mistakes. The first and greatest had been to imagine that a flaming political issue could be quenched by calling it a "legal" issue and deciding it judicially.

But the notion that the Court could legitimately co-operate with the "political" branches in dealing with such an issue was almost equally self-destructive, for the Court's claim to public regard rested heavily on the belief that its work was distinguishable from "politics." In 1850 the Court enjoyed popular support as nearly unanimous as can ever be expected in a diverse democratic society. It was playing a modest but significant part in the affairs of the nation. Eight years later, it had forfeited that position, and its role in the American polity was nearly negligible. Taney and his fellows had been almost irresistibly provoked to do what they did in the *Dred Scott* case; the Chief's errors were well intended and understandable; he does not deserve the infamy that was so long associated with his name, for he was during most of his tenure a wise and good leader of the Court. But the fact that he had these virtues does not make his errors in this case any the less woeful; the fact that the Court under him had reached the pinnacle of its historic prestige merely heightens the tragedy of its decline.

The extent of that tragedy is revealed by the peculiar transvaluation of values that took place in connection with the case of *Ableman* v. *Booth* in 1859. Ableman, a Milwaukee editor, had assisted a fugitive slave to escape from federal custody, and was therefore arrested for violation of the national Fugitive Slave Law. The Wisconsin Supreme Court ordered him released on a writ of habeas corpus, and the order was obeyed. However, the national government then appealed to the Supreme Court of the United States, which held that the state courts had no business to interfere with the conduct of federal law and that the Fugitive Slave Law was constitutional.

Now the first point was of course the very keystone of the Supreme Court's jurisdictional arch; this was the principle for which Marshall had fought so shrewdly and effectively. If the national government and its judicial arm can operate only by the leave of the several states, the nation is not a nation and the Supreme Court is not a supreme court. Yet the decision was violently attacked, the state was urged to resist, the cry that the Court had no power thus to overrule a state was heard, not only in Wisconsin, but throughout the North.

This was the doctrine of nullification, familiar since the Virginia and Kentucky resolutions of 1798–99, re-energized by the mordant genius of Calhoun in 1832, and now becoming an article of faith below the Mason-Dixon line. That it should be invoked by a northern state as a challenge to the Court is a measure of the witless inconsistency of some Northern opinion but is also a measure of judicial bankruptcy. The Court's effective existence depended on acceptance of the principle of national authority, and there was no hope that this principle would be entertained in the South one minute after an anti-slavery opinion was rendered. The judicial constituency had always been drawn from those who had a stake in nationalism, and in 1859 that meant the North. But the monumental indiscretion of *Dred Scott* had forfeited Northern allegiance. For the first time in its history, the Court seemed almost friendless (for the fair-weather friendship of the South provided very cold comfort).

DECLINE WITHOUT FALL

The gloomy view of the judiciary's estate that is suggested by these events seems confirmed when we glance briefly at the Court's vicissitudes during the war years that followed. War is never a favorable environment for judicial power. It is characterized by emotion and quick, drastic action; and courts are not well equipped to cope with either. But natural handicaps are not enough to account for the impotency of the Supreme Court during the Civil War. It was of course, necessarily, the court of the Union, for the Confederacy was going its own way. But a substantial proportion of Union opinion associated the Court with the Confederate cause, unfairly but nonetheless stubbornly. It was hardly to be expected that its mandates would be eagerly sought or greatly heeded.

Taney, the luckless scapegoat of this judicial ice age, added another item to the Unionist score against him when less than three months after Lincoln's inauguration, he challenged the President's power to suspend the writ of habeas corpus for wartime purposes. He ordered that John Merryman, a Maryland secessionist being held in military prison, be brought before him on the writ, and when the commanding general refused to comply, Taney ordered that the general himself be haled into court in order to be fined and imprisoned for his disobedience. The marshal seeking to carry out this assignment was denied admission to the fort by the general, and Taney addressed himself to the President, calling on Lincoln to "perform his constitutional duty." The President did not reply. The only immediate reward for Taney's zeal was another shower of venom from the Northern press against this "hoary apologist for treason."

The Court under Taney

The Chief's point was in fact pretty well taken. Lincoln had wielded executive power somewhat recklessly during those early months of hostilities. It is at least doubtful that the President alone had the power to suspend the writ of habeas corpus, and it was not unreasonable to ask that he get congressional approval before he did so. But any chance that the Court might play the role of a moderating force, holding the government within sensible boundaries as it waged the bloody war, had been squandered in 1857.

And the Court majority knew it. Taney's willingness in the *Merryman* case to add to the judicial sea of troubles was not characteristic of the Court as a whole while the shooting continued. The judges found reason to refuse jurisdiction on cases involving such ticklish questions as the trial of civilians by military commission and the Legal Tender Acts. A decision adverse to the Union government in either might well have brought the temple crashing about their ears. The Court also upheld the power of the President to make war in the legal sense without waiting for a congressional declaration. Surely, it might be said, the day of the Supreme Court as a powerful factor in America was done. The Civil War was not only testing whether the nation could long endure; it was also demonstrating that the experiment of an independent and influential national judiciary had failed. The aged Chief Justice was not alone in believing that the Court would never "be restored to the authority and rank which the Constitution intended to confer on it," that is, the status it had attained under Marshall and himself.

But like Marshall, who died with similar forebodings weighing on his spirit, Taney and his colleagues had built better than he knew. On the foundation Marshall had bequeathed, the Taney

99

Court had fashioned a system of jurisprudence and a judicial image; and the nation had learned to accept one and to admire the other. The judges had maintained a clear line of connection between Marshall's doctrines and their own. This was wise because it preserved the essential idea of the fundamental law as a steady river of continuity in otherwise capricious political seas. They had used the judicial veto, and this was important because it not only kept the notion of constitutional limit alive but reminded those who might forget that judicial sovereignty had not atrophied. But their discipleship to Marshall was discriminating; the veto had been handled discreetly; the Taney judges were aware that both the economic and the political world had changed since Marshall's time. They had managed to strike a middle ground that reconciled the American will for change with the desire for order and stability, the American's wish to have his way with his respect for the rule of law. Their reward had been the homage of the nation.

This achievement had been endangered by the audacious assumption in *Dred Scott* that the judiciary could solve the major problem facing America. But the public habit of reverence was strongly ingrained by those years of painstaking cultivation, and not even this calamity could stamp it out altogether. How many such adversities the judiciary could sustain is another question. The fact is that this wound, though grievous, was not fatal. The qualities of the American mind that had made the Court of the past possible had not disappeared. Americans, so to speak, had needed the Supreme Court to help express their own peculiar medley of governmental aspirations. When the war was over that need would reawaken.

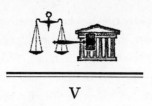

V

Constitutional Evolution in the
Gilded Age: 1865-1900

In the opening chapters of this volume it was suggested that the Civil War marks the close of one great epoch in the history of judicial review, and the beginning of another. For the Court, as for many individuals, the war wrought profound changes both internal and external, changes so basic that it might well take decades to realize their dimensions. No person or institution or nation that had endured that experience could ever be the same as before; men like Henry Adams, who had lived abroad during the conflagration, were astonished—and somewhat appalled—when they returned to see the altered America that had emerged from the flames. And the judges of the Supreme Court, though lacking, perhaps, Adams' peculiar gifts of detachment and insight, had equal reason to rub their eyes. Their constitutional universe had been similarly transfigured.

For one thing, the nation-state problem had changed its nature dramatically. The Marshall and Taney Courts had been perennially haunted by the danger that centrifugal forces would tear the nation apart, and their jurisprudence had been shaped with that terrible threat always in mind. The Northern victory scotched this bugbear; when Chief Justice Chase declared in 1868 that ours was "an indestructible Union, composed of indestructible States," he spoke with a just confidence unknown to his predecessors.

The second great difference between the old constitutional environment and the new was slower to reveal itself fully but in the long run even more important to the future of judicial review. It was, of course, that capitalism, developing at a rapid but relatively moderate tempo in prewar years, had been given an enormous accelerating thrust by the war and was now proceeding at a pace of headlong expansion that was unexampled in the nation's history. The agrarian nation Jefferson and Marshall had known was now the industrial-mercantile nation that Hamilton had envisioned. The change had not really occurred overnight; in the 1850's this metamorphosis had been clearly enough foreshadowed. But in the 1850's the problems of slavery and the Union had claimed a very heavy share of attention from those who had thought about constitutional questions, and the constitutional implications of the rise of capitalism were correspondingly obscured. Now those implications were evident and were soon to be unavoidable. In 1866 the judges faced what was in effect a new judicial environment; and it was getting newer all the time.

For as capitalism expanded, it impinged on the lives of individuals as never before; as it became the most important fact in American life, it became the most troublesome fact as well. Men began to say, first from scattered quarters, then in a steadily augmenting chorus, that the power of government should be used to control this giant, to mitigate the harm to individual and collective welfare that it might do if left unchecked. And, conversely, others began to say, with a vehemence and volume far greater than in the past, that the giant would serve the community best if it were allowed to go its own way, that governmental tinkering with the economy was both futile and mischievous, that laissez faire should be the watchword of the day. The question of whether government should control capitalism, and how much it should control it, moved to the center of the American political arena and was never very far from that center for the next seventy years.

The results of all this for judicial review in the postwar era were several, but the most significant was that the Court's focus of interest was radically modified. The dominant interest of the Court in the past had been the nation-state relationship, and the dominant judicial value, as I have said earlier, was the preservation of the Union. The war did not of course obliterate the nation-state issue, for that issue is interminable in a federal republic. But its importance in the judicial order of things became much less, both absolutely because the very existence of the Union no longer hung in the balance and relatively because the greater issue of economic control had arisen to dominate the political scene. The postwar Court was no more disposed to leave the question of economic control alone than Marshall was disposed to leave the question of federalism alone. He had taught his successors to view themselves as vital factors in the governmental process, he had tried within the limits of judicial capacity to guide and coerce America along paths of his choosing. Whether or not he had succeeded in all his aims, he had at any rate succeeded in planting a judicial tradition of mentorship. The judges who now began coming to the Court—

men like Chase and Bradley and Field—felt authorized to help America decide what kind of nation it should be. And since the gravest problem facing America was government regulation of business, that problem gradually became the major interest of America's constitutional court.

But if the Court's tradition helps explain why it was likely to focus now on the economic control issue, the tradition is also useful in predicting where the judges' preferences would lie in the evolving conflict between the proponents of control and of laissez faire. Marshall's darlings had been the nation and the property-owner, and most Supreme Court judges between 1789 and 1860 had shared these twin affections to a greater or lesser degree. Now that the national government had vindicated its existence in trial by battle, its health seemed reasonably assured, and it no longer required the solicitous protection of the Court. But the property-owner (that is, the businessman) began in the 1870's to be harried by government; "legislation by clamor," in William Graham Sumner's phrase, threatened to penalize him and hamper his freedom of action—to prevent him, as his admirers saw it, from helping the community by helping himself. A Court committed by its tradition to the cause of property rights, composed of judges who were inevitably drawn largely from the ranks of the "haves" and who were of course by definition lawyers and thus imbued with the conservative bias that has always characterized the American legal fraternity —such a Court was almost certain to throw its weight against the regulatory movement and on the side of the business community.

In this second great period of constitutional history, then, running roughly from the end of the Civil War to 1937, the major interest of the Supreme Court as a molder of governmental policy became the relationship between government and business; and the major value of the Court (to carry on the terminology used in earlier chapters) was the protection of the business community against government. The nation-state relationship, once salient, was now subordinate; the fear that the states would wound or destroy the nation was replaced by the fear that government, state or national, would unduly hinder business in its mission to make America wealthy and wise.

But to say this is the beginning of analysis, not the end. Historians like Charles Beard and J. Allen Smith and Brooks Adams were telling us, as early as the first decade of the twentieth century, that the Supreme Court was remarkably friendly to the pleas of "vested wealth." Those who at first recoiled in horror from such a suggestion have now generally subsided, and the fact has been incorporated among the standard assumptions of students of the era. The challenging question is not whether the Court of 1865–1937 favored the business community but what was the nature and degree of that favoritism, how was it implemented, to what extent was it qualified and self-restrained? In short, what role did the Court work out for itself in the light of its new interests and values? As suggested earlier in this volume, the Court's whole history can be viewed as a constant, or at least repeated, readjustment of role to suit the circumstances of each succeeding judicial era. What were the readjustment problems faced by the Court in this new age of burgeoning capitalism and regulatory government? How did the Court meet them?

The historical record that supplies the answers to these questions can be divided into two subperiods, the first extending roughly from the Civil War to 1900, the second ending with a bang and a good many whimpers in the fateful spring of 1937.

And it is of course the first of these subperiods that concerns us for the remainder of this chapter.

An unwary reader, examining the behavior of the Court in the early postwar years, might easily get the impression that the foregoing paragraphs exaggerate the predominance of the government-business relationship in this judicial era. For some time after the shooting ended, the Court was heavily concerned with after-echoes of the war and with the knotty problem of Reconstruction for the conquered South. These issues were imposing enough in their own right to preoccupy the minds of the judges, and it would not be surprising if the Court had concentrated on them exclusively. But the significant fact is that even in the thick of these postwar difficulties the problem of economic control persists in peeping through; even while the guns are still reverberating or the "bloody shirt of the Rebellion" being most violently waved, the judicial opinions hint strongly of a quite different world which the judges themselves are perhaps as yet only dimly aware of.

True, there are few such hints in the decisions involving the war-engendered problem of military trials. In 1862, President Lincoln had authorized military commanders to seize and try by military tribunal civilians who engaged in "disloyal practices," even in areas remote from the actual conflict where the civil courts were duly functioning. Although in fact this authority was used quite sparingly, in principle it represented a startling transgression on individual rights, and the executive order was bitterly criticized in some quarters.

However, in 1863 it was applied in Ohio by General Burnside

to the notorious "Copperhead" Clement L. Vallandigham who had, in a public meeting, denounced the "wicked, cruel, and unnecessary" war and had urged resistance to such extraordinary powers as those granted by the presidential order. Burnside promptly arrested him, presumably under that very order, and a military commission, finding him guilty of aiding and comforting the enemy, sentenced him to detention for the balance of the war.

Then Lincoln, apparently somewhat embarrassed by Burnside's zeal and always alert to the opportunity for a jest, commuted the sentence and ordered Vallandigham sent into Southern territory, where he could be free to comfort rebels to his heart's content. Meanwhile the prisoner had applied for a writ of habeas corpus to the United States circuit court in Cincinnati, and the writ had been denied. He and his supporters wished of course to pursue the issue to the Supreme Court in the hope that the Lincoln administration might be declared to have acted illegally. But the approach they chose, seemingly on the assumption that it was the only way now available, was to petition that the Supreme Court call up the record of the military commission for review by a writ of certiorari. This writ was, and is, a standard form by which the Court exercises control over inferior tribunals, but the use of the writ is confined by law to certain types of cases. The Court held, quite rightly, that its powers of review consisted only of those granted by the Constitution and Congress, and that it had not been authorized by either of those agents to call up the proceedings of a military commission in this way. Vallandigham was left to seek his satisfaction elsewhere, and he did, running for governor of Ohio in 1864 and polling nearly 40 per cent of the total vote.

The members of the Court may well have thanked providence

for the jurisdictional technicalities that removed Vallandigham's cause from their ken, for the scars of the *Dred Scott* decision were as yet by no means healed, and a "pro-Copperhead" decision would not have been received kindly by Unionist opinion. However, in 1866, when *Ex Parte Milligan* came before them, the fighting was over, and the judges felt that a backward slap at the wartime military trials was now in order. In 1864, Lambdin P. Milligan, a citizen of Indiana, had played a leading part in a plot by the Order of the Sons of Liberty to set free prisoners of war and take over by armed force the state governments in Indiana, Ohio, and Illinois. He had been tried by a military tribunal and sentenced to hang. Milligan, like Vallandigham, then asked the circuit court in Indianapolis for a writ of habeas corpus.

So far the cases of Vallandigham and Milligan would appear to be kindred in all important respects. But from the viewpoint of the Supreme Court when it received Milligan's appeal, there were two significant differences. For one thing, a law of March 3, 1863, though suspending the privilege of the writ of habeas corpus, had provided that if a grand jury had met after a man was taken into custody and had failed to indict him, the prisoner could require the court concerned to order his release. This seemed to give the circuit court undoubted authority to hear Milligan's case, and moreover it strongly suggested that Congress had tacitly forbidden military trial if the civil courts were open and grand juries were duly being assembled. The circuit court to which Milligan applied professed doubts on these and other points and passed the issues up to the Supreme Court by the process known as "certification." This mode of appellate jurisdiction is provided in the Judiciary Act, and thus the jurisdictional difficulties that barred the way in the case of Vallandigham did not arise. The question of the validity of the military trials was clearly and regularly before the Court.

The second difference between the two cases was of course that the war had ended by the time Milligan's case reached the Supreme Court. Some commentators have made more of this point than is warranted, suggesting that the Court gratuitously seized upon a technicality to escape jurisdiction in the first case because the atmosphere was supercharged with danger for a Court that presumed to interfere with the conduct of the war. As we have seen, there was nothing gratuitous about it; in order to reach Vallandigham's case, the judges would have had to invent jurisdiction that was not provided by law. But this is not to say that they were unaware of the difference between the military trial question in 1863 and in 1866. Their awareness shows in a contrast of the spirits of the two decisions, the cautious opinion of Justice Wayne in the first case, restricting himself to the jurisdictional issue, eschewing any implications about the propriety of such trials, and the boldly venturesome majority opinion in *Milligan*, suggesting with oratorical flourishes that the Court was now ready to resume its place as a leading participant in the councils of the nation.

A majority of five now felt prepared to say that no one, not even Congress, could authorize military trial of civilians when the civil courts were still open. The remaining four judges were not willing to go so far, but they concurred that Congress, though possessing the power to authorize military trials in war, had not exerted it here, and that Milligan must go free. Justice Davis' majority opinion is the more remarkable in that he not only deals with an issue unnecessary to the decision (for he agrees that Congress had not authorized the trial, and the question of whether it could have done so is thus hypothetical) but intrepidly asserts, in effect, that the Supreme Court is the final judge of what constitutes military necessity.

This is not the Court of the wartime years, smarting under the lash of criticism that had immediately followed *Dred Scott*, modestly forbearing from interference in the great affairs of state. It has shown itself willing to wait until the national temperature has dropped somewhat below the boiling point, but there is no mistaking the intimation, made as soon as that stage of excessive peril is past, that the Court is moving back to its accustomed seat of power as fast as circumstances will allow. There is no danger that America will be deprived of judicial guidance in coping with the problems that the postwar era has in store.

Unfortunately one of those problems, though temporary, was calculated to generate almost as much heat as the war itself. This was the problem of Reconstruction in the South, for the Republican party, now riding high, was determined upon a policy of revenge and self-perpetuation. To those ends Congress had divided the South into military districts under military commanders and had provided for military trials in the areas at the commanders' discretion. Under the rule of the *Milligan* case such trials were plainly invalid, but in that case the Court had been looking back at a situation in the past, and now it was looking squarely at a present danger.

The enemies of Reconstruction hastened to bring up a case that would force the Court to stand on the *Milligan* logic and declare the Reconstruction Acts unconstitutional, but they encountered a series of jurisdictional checks. A request for an injunction to prevent Johnson from enforcing the laws was turned down on the ground that an injunction could not lie against the President. Similar suits against the Secretary of War and military officials encountered from the Court the declaration that they presented "political questions" (that is, abstract questions of sovereignty rather than the immediate question of whether John Doe was being deprived of particular rights) and were not justiciable. The would-be litigants seemed on the point of success in *Ex Parte McCardle*, involving a Mississippi editor arrested by a military commander, for his right to appeal in a habeas corpus proceeding seemed clearly guaranteed by federal law. But the Court delayed action until Congress itself provided a checkmate by passing a bill that deprived the Court of the jurisdiction under which McCardle's cause had been brought. The Court unanimously—and, we may guess, thankfully—held that this act was valid, that Congress' power over appellate jurisdiction was plenary. And the upshot was that the Reconstruction Acts, though palpably unconstitutional under the *Milligan* doctrine, were never tested in the Supreme Court.

THE COURT'S NEW SPIRIT AND THE LEGAL TENDER ISSUE

The generalizations that can be drawn from the military trial cases are two. The first is that the postwar Court is wary of involving itself in issues so emotionally charged that a decision might precipitate ruthless counterattack from the dominant political forces of the nation. But the second is that, with this caveat duly in mind, the judges still feel it their right and duty to help America decide the fundamental issues that confront it. An understanding of the delicate distinction that is here implied is crucial to an understanding of the Court's historic place in American life. The Court tacitly acknowledges an informal but very real limit on its jurisdiction: the most explosive issues are "non-justiciable." Sometimes (as in war) the most explosive issues will also be the most "important," and then the Court is likely to play a rather modest role in national affairs. But this modesty is brought on by knowledge of the explosiveness of the question rather than by awe at its importance. Neither Marshall nor his predecessors nor his successors have, until lately at any rate, displayed much diffidence about substituting their judgment for that of others when the moment for doing so seemed auspicious. But they have displayed a fairly consistent awareness that for everything on earth there is a season.

The willingness of the postwar Court to remount the heights of power, foreshadowed in the *Milligan* case, is further illustrated in a series of other cases involving problems of war and Reconstruction. And now the King Charles's head of economic control does begin to break through the more immediate judicial preoccupations.

Perhaps the most ambitious, though abortive, of these early postwar ventures into judicial supervision was the attempt to adjudicate the weighty issue of legal tender. During the war the Union government, being in some fiscal difficulties, had issued $450,000,000 in "greenbacks" (that is, paper money which was not redeemable in coin and thus owed its value, if any, to the government's declaration that it was legal tender for "payment of all debts, public and private"). The question of whether Congress had power to issue such fiat money and compel creditors to accept it was an old one, and a case (*Roosevelt* v. *Meyer*) challenging the law's validity reached the Supreme Court in 1863. But the Court escaped jurisdiction by the simple, if inexcusable expedient of misreading the Judiciary Act in such a way as to prohibit a Supreme Court hearing. We must assume either that the judges were unfamiliar with the law that furnishes their very basis for being, or that they deliberately chose a Pickwickian interpretation in order to avoid deciding, in wartime, a question so central to the conduct of the war. It is hard to think of a third reasonable explanation.

At any rate this decision postponed the constitutional issue of legal tender, as *Vallandigham* had postponed the war trials issue, until the war was over. Even then the Court approached the matter cautiously, avoiding constitutional problems by strict construction of the statutes, agreeing that Congress had power to issue greenbacks, but not grappling with the ultimate question, which was whether creditors must accept them. However, in 1869 this question was squarely presented by a creditor who refused to take payment in paper for a debt contracted in 1860, before the passage of the Legal Tender Acts. And in 1870 a Court majority held in *Hepburn* v. *Griswold* that the refusal was justified because the law, at least as applied to debts contracted before its passage, was unconstitutional.

Chief Justice Chase's opinion for the majority has been roundly criticized by generations of observers, not only on the ground that it undertook to argue and decide a question inappropriate for judicial treatment, but also on the ground that the Chief Justice failed to make a good case for the point of view he did adopt. His argument was that the legal tender requirement was not a "necessary and proper" means of carrying out the war powers, and this involved him in an essentially economic treatise on the evils of soft money, hardly a matter that falls within the range of judicial expertness. He further sought to prop up this slender reed of logic by contending that the law violated the "spirit" of the Constitution because it was unjust; and the letter as well because, by decreasing the value of the creditor's accounts receivable, it took money without "due process of law."

The noteworthy things about the decision from the viewpoint of this chapter are that it illustrates, as *Milligan* did, the postwar Court's eagerness to impose its wisdom on the government in connection with momentous issues, and more particularly a growing compulsion to defend property rights against all who might assail them. The question at stake was the power of the national government to control its own currency, a power which, as Justice Bradley was to say, may be "absolutely essential to independent national existence." The audacity of the Court's decision to restrict this authority by its own fiat is breathtaking when we consider that the *Dred Scott* case lay only thirteen years in the past. And the invocation of the due process clause, though it seems a kind of afterthought here, is prophetic. For it was by way of this clause that the Court was ultimately to claim the overlordship of economic policy that is asserted so daringly, though lamely, in the *Hepburn* case.

But the *Hepburn* doctrine itself, including its novel gloss of due process, enjoyed the shortest life of any important doctrine ever promulgated by the Court. Justice Grier, who helped to make up the five-man majority, had retired before the decision was announced, and on the very day of announcement President Grant nominated two new justices, Strong and Bradley, to bring the Court to its full complement of nine. The *Hepburn* vote had been on strict party lines—five Democrats against the law (counting Chase who was busily becoming a Democrat at this time) and three Republicans for. The two new appointees were of course Republicans and could presumably be counted on to uphold the Legal Tender Acts, if they got a chance to do so. They helped to provide that chance by voting to accept jurisdiction in two cases which raised an issue similar to *Hepburn* and agreeing to reconsider the constitutional issue. And in 1871, only fifteen months after *Hepburn,* a new majority held that the Acts were constitutional in all respects (the *Legal Tender Cases*). Thus Chief Justice Chase's tortured logic and his doubtful interpretations of constitutional doctrine died in infancy. But the spirit of his opinion—the implied superiority of judicial wisdom, the insistence that no issue is too big or too intricate for judicial governance, the solicitude for the aggrieved possessing class—these lived on in decisions of the future, as we shall see.

THE FOURTEENTH AMENDMENT AND THE

SLAUGHTERHOUSE CASES

The *Legal Tender Cases* then blended the motifs of war and Reconstruction with the more purely economic themes that were to dominate the Court's value system in the near future. Somewhat the same qualities were apparent in the *Slaughter-House Cases* of 1873, one of the great landmarks in American constitutional history. But here the harmonies were even more complicated, for the eternal issue of federalism could also be detected, running through the opinions and influencing their result.

The cases involved the Fourteenth Amendment, the second and, as it turned out, most pregnant of the three major constitutional changes that had been imposed by the triumphant Republicans on the nation in general and the defeated South in particular. In its first section the Amendment declared that:

No State shall make or enforce any law which shall abridge the privileges or immunities of citizens of the United States; nor shall any State deprive any person of life, liberty, or property, without due process of law; nor deny to any person within its jurisdiction the equal protection of the laws.

115

This sentence, especially in its last two clauses, was to become perhaps the most adjudicated and discussed sentence in the federal Constitution, but in 1873 its meaning was uncertain and its significance highly conjectural. In order to understand both its future importance and its contemporary ambiguity, we must glance backward again at pre–Civil War constitutional history.

For one thing it must be realized that the Bill of Rights (Amendments I–VIII) had been held to limit the federal government alone, not the states. This was Marshall's doctrine in *Barron* v. *Baltimore* (1833); it had never been seriously controverted; the states could therefore infringe on individual liberties as they willed, except for relatively mild restrictions like the contract clause or the ex post facto clause. The second point worth special note is that the due process clause, which appears in both the Fifth Amendment as a limit on the nation and in the Fourteenth as a limit on the states, had usually been interpreted as having only a procedural meaning. That is, it did not prevent government from depriving a person of life, liberty, or property, but simply guaranteed that certain standard procedures would be observed before a person was so deprived. In this sense the concept of due process did not import a very strict curb on governmental power, for it meant that only the *manner*, not the *object*, of legislation was subject to judicial scrutiny. And yet having said this, we must also admit that the difference between manner and object, between procedure and substance, is not always so clear-cut in practice as it may appear in conception, and that there had existed for some time an undercurrent of feeling that the due process requirement could be, and perhaps should be, enlarged into a general prohibition against "unjust" or "arbitrary" legislation. Such a prohibition, if recognized, could now apply to both the national government and the states through the Fifth and Fourteenth Amendments, respectively.

These two points lead to a question or rather a series of them: what was the quoted sentence of the Fourteenth Amendment designed to accomplish? Was it intended to reverse *Barron* v. *Baltimore* and make the Bill of Rights applicable to the states, that is, were the "privileges or immunities" it speaks of those that have heretofore been protected against national action alone by the Bill of Rights (free speech, jury trial, etc.)? Was the due process clause merely meant to outlaw unfair legal procedures in the states or to forbid all governmental action infringing on property which a court might regard as unjust? Was the "equal protection" clause to be taken literally? Did it mean that the states' laws could enforce no discriminations at all between persons? If the sentence meant all of these things, or even a substantial part of them, then the federal system had been drastically revised, for the whole domain of civil rights now fell under the protection of the national judiciary.

Unfortunately these questions are easier to state than to answer. The best evidence is that the Congress that passed, and the state legislators who ratified, the Amendment had extremely mixed or extremely vague ideas about the meaning of these terms. Only the query about due process can be answered with anything resembling confidence: it is most unlikely that those who participated in establishing the Amendment expected it to protect property in a broad way from all forms of state-imposed injustice, for the phrase had usually been construed much more narrowly. Yet even here there is a modicum of doubt, and with respect to the other clauses the doubt becomes full-fledged confusion.

However, as has been remarked earlier in this volume, am-

biguity of constitutional language and uncertainty about con-
stitution-makers' intent is the very *sine qua non* of judicial review as it has operated in the United States. The Court itself
could not have been the institution it was if the framers in 1789
had spoken more plainly about the judicial power. Great clauses
like the commerce clause and the contract clause could not have
been shaped to the judicial purpose if they had been drawn
more precisely. It is arguable that the Fourteenth Amendment
was a kind of license for the Court to proceed at will within
broad limits, to make of these phrases what it felt was right
and feasible. That is, after all, what the Court had done with
other imprecise mandates. If the framers of the Fourteenth
wanted their brainchild to be treated otherwise, nothing would
have been easier than for them to say so. They did not, and
their failure to clarify their intentions provided the Court with
a golden opportunity to inaugurate a new era in the history of
judicial review.

Now to return to the *Slaughter-House Cases.* In 1869, a
"carpetbag" legislature in Louisiana had passed a law granting
a monopoly in the slaughtering of livestock to a single New
Orleans corporation. Other New Orleans butchers were understandably outraged by this invasion of their occupational freedom, but under traditional interpretations of the Constitution
it seemed that they would be forced to grin and bear it unless
the legislature could be persuaded to change its mind. The prewar Constitution would have offered the Supreme Court no
way to redress their grievance, even if it had the will to do so,
for the states' control of such economic matters had been recognized as plenary so long as the contract clause was not violated.

But now the butchers had two new cards to play. The first
was the Fourteenth Amendment ratified in 1868 and hence ap-

plicable to the legislation. And the second was the Honorable John A. Campbell, one-time Supreme Court justice and now one of the greatly successful lawyers of the day. There was a saying, "Leave it to God and Mr. Campbell," and the butchers gladly put their case in the hands of those high authorities. Mr. Campbell rose to the occasion with a lengthy, scholarly, and powerful argument that the Fourteenth Amendment had revolutionized the American system by bringing the rights of man, including of course the right to occupational freedom, under national judicial protection. Already, in 1873, he was showing the Court the way to provide business with relief from governmental meddling: the Fourteenth Amendment had enacted the principle of laissez faire into the American Constitution.

The Court was visibly shaken by this brilliant improvisation, but a majority was not quite convinced. Five to four, through Justice Miller, it rejected the butchers' claims. The "privileges or immunities" clause, said Miller, does not secure against state action the great basic rights that are protected against national action by the Bill of Rights. It refers only to certain special rights of national citizenship, such as the right to travel freely about the country, the "right to use the navigable waters of the United States," etc. The freedoms guaranteed against national action by the Bill of Rights are at the mercy of the states, just as they have been since *Barron* v. *Baltimore*. As for the argument that the due process clause accomplished Mr. Campbell's aims, it is not sustained by any "construction of that phrase that we have ever seen, or any that we deem admissible." And as for the equal protection clause, it is clearly a provision to protect the Negroes in their newly won freedom and has no applications to the case in hand.

One interesting thing about this decision is the contrast between what it seemed to do and what it actually did. It seemed to slam the door on the question of whether the Amendment had radically altered the federal relationship, and on the sub-question of whether property rights were to be granted broad national protection. The answers, one might think, were both emphatically "no." But, in the event, the decision turned out to mean only that these two great developments were postponed until the magical process of "judicial inclusion and exclusion" could bring them about more subtly and gradually. Outright acceptance of Campbell's argument would have imposed upon the Court the vast and perhaps unmanageable problem of protecting all civil rights against state abridgment; moreover, it would have left the Court small room to maneuver, to feel its way toward self-chosen goals within the limits of the politically possible. While seeming to dash all hopes for a constitutional check of this sort, Miller had actually made it possible for the American constitutional system to evolve, as it always has, by slow "Burkean" accretions rather than by a single great mutation; and he had left the Court free to define, as it had in the past, its own role in the national polity.

Moreover, this process of closing the door but leaving it unbolted served another purpose, probably unsuspected by Justice Miller, but nonetheless important in the Court's dawning future. It helped to consign the redoubtable problem of Negro rights to a rather trivial place in the judicial agenda and thus removed an incumbrance that might have been most troublesome. With nicely mingled idealism and opportunism, the victorious Republicans had forced through not only the "War Amendments" (XIII, XIV, XV) but a series of "civil rights acts" designed to secure the Negroes in their newly won privileges of citizenship. Miller's narrow definition of "privileges or immunities" disposed of any likelihood that that constitutional clause would help the freedmen. And a few years later the national civil rights acts were emasculated by the holding that the "enforcement clause" of the Fourteenth Amendment did not authorize Congress to legislate against transgression by private persons on the rights of individuals, Negro or white. This left only the due process and equal protection clauses which Miller had brushed aside so disrespectfully and which for a good many years were to play little part in insuring such meager privileges as the Negro enjoyed. Outright and flagrant state discriminations based on race might be struck down by the judicial arm, but indirect and informal distinctions were tolerated, and legally enforced segregation of races was permitted so long as the facilities provided were "substantially equal" (the adverb was generously construed). And of course, except in very special circumstances, the discriminatory behavior of private persons was beyond the reach of the courts and Congress alike. The judges thus avoided the distractions and the diffusion of energy that might have hampered them, if they had chosen to defend both the businessman and the Negro at the same time.

THE DRIFT TOWARD CONSTITUTIONAL LAISSEZ FAIRE

Now, and to an increasing degree as war and Reconstruction recede into the past, the Court's history becomes a history of response to the advance of what was later to be called "the general-welfare state." The development of this preoccupation is foreshadowed, as I have suggested, in such immediately post-war decisions as *Hepburn* and in the opinions of *Slaughter-House* dissenters like Field and Bradley. Whether they were more prescient than their majority associates or simply more passionately devoted to the defense of property, the fact is that these judges were ready in 1873 to interpret the Fourteenth Amendment as a general restriction on economic legislation.

But the Court majority was more hesitant, and for good reasons. For one thing, some, like Justice Miller, were undoubtedly disturbed by the enormity of the assignment Mr. Campbell had urged upon them. Miller may have been, as his biographer says, more "reconciled to the exercise of power by the political branches of government" than most of his colleagues, but others probably shared some of his misgivings and had to be won over gradually to the radical construction espoused by Bradley and Field. For another thing, it is probably true that the judges in 1873 had not yet become fully alert to the nature and extent of the welfare state "menace." The Granger Movement, an attack on corporate autonomy and especially the railroads, was already under way in the Midwest; but it was still possible in 1873 to view such developments as atypical, temporary, and therefore only mildly alarming. The specter of full-fledged paternal government, of state socialism, had already begun to haunt the dreams of Field, but others still slept fairly soundly.

And finally, as I have intimated, traditional legal doctrine hindered the program of judicial empire-building that Mr. Campbell proposed. The states had always been allowed a pretty free hand to regulate economic affairs under their reserved "police power." The Marshall-Taney view of national power under the "necessary and proper" clause had been uniformly permissive. The term "privileges and immunities" had reposed innocuously in Article IV of the Constitution since 1789, and no court had forced it to bear the weight of implications that

Campbell now suggested. Due process had been regarded chiefly as a procedural guarantee.

In these early postwar years, then, and partly for these reasons, the majority seemed willing, if not entirely content, to leave economic affairs to the "political branches of government." The self-denial of the majority in *Slaughter-House* was matched in 1869 by *Paul* v. *Virginia*, sustaining state regulation of the insurance business and as late as 1879 by *Stone* v. *Mississippi*, which held that the state could prohibit lotteries, even when conducted by a corporation that had formerly enjoyed a state-chartered right to do so. Corporate charters are protected by the contract clause but, said the Court, this protection is subject to the implied qualification that "the public health or public morals" cannot be bargained away; that is, in these fields the state can change its mind and retract privileges it has previously granted.

These decisions, and others that might be cited, do suggest a judicial temper that was temporarily tolerant toward some forms of state interference with property rights. But as the years passed this indulgent mood became harder and harder for the Court to sustain and the threat of economic control became more real and more perturbing. Little by little the urge to intrude in economic affairs waxed stronger and stronger, the desire of Field and Bradley, expressed in *Slaughter-House*, was converted into the desire of the Court as a whole. By 1880 the majority was coming fully alive to the danger of economic control and to the need for some judicial action that would check it.

However, at this point, as I have suggested, the Court was handicapped in assuming this weighty but attractive assignment by its own inherited legal traditions. The judges had the will but not the way to protect business against what Joseph Choate was to call, in 1895, the "onward march of communism." What they needed was the due process clause in its 1900 form; what they had was the vague and relatively feeble clause of the Anglo-American legal tradition.

Their willingness to take to the ramparts on behalf of laissez faire is made clear enough in the decisions involving the commerce clause. When the weapons were at hand the judges were ready to use them. In this field, it will be remembered, the Court had available the doctrine of federal pre-emption (see pp. 85–86), drawn from such old decisions as *Gibbons* v. *Ogden* and *Cooley* v. *Board of Wardens;* and it was relatively easy to find state economic regulations invalid because they encroached on interstate commerce. The Court proceeded to do so in a series of decisions running in a seldom broken line from the year of Chief Justice Waite's appointment (1874) to the turn of the century. The states' power to tax interstate business activity was seriously impaired in such decisions as the *Philadelphia and Reading Rail Road* case in 1873, which outlawed freight tonnage taxes on interstate shipments; and other state attempts to control business within their borders fell under a similar ban in the 1870's. Perhaps the most important of these early decisions was the *Pensacola Telegraph* case in 1877, which precluded the states from granting telegraph monopolies, but it is only one of several. The rise of the regulatory movement was bringing commerce cases to the Court in growing numbers, and the judges were giving notice that state laws in this field would be scrutinized with a sharp eye.

This promise was honored with increasing consistency as time went on. There were some fourteen cases between 1877 and 1886 in which state regulations of commerce were held invalid, most of them on the ground that the subject in question was national in character and required a uniform rule which only Congress could provide. Nor does this include the most far-reaching of all, the *Wabash* case in 1886 which effectively forbade the states to regulate interstate railroad rates. And after this date, the tempo of such decisions increased still further; the states' power to tax and regulate business was more and more constrained by the doctrine that national commerce must be nationally controlled, if it is to be controlled at all.

Charles Warren, in his admirable history of the Supreme Court, describes Waite's tenure (1874–88) in terms of the ebb and flow of "nationalism." The non-nationalist period runs through 1880; thereafter nationalist tendencies begin to display themselves. The fact that the pre-1880 Court struck down a healthy number of state laws under the *Cooley* rule is apparently viewed as an enigmatic exception to its general attitude of tolerance toward state regulations, and that tolerance is otherwise evidenced by the judiciary's willingness to leave to the states the problem of Negro rights and by its failure in these years to use the Fourteenth Amendment to invalidate state business regulations.

This analysis mistakes the secondary for the primary. Of course the judges had opinions on the subject of nationalism, and they were growing increasingly aware during this period that business was becoming national in character. Truly intrastate commercial activity was far less common than it had been; more and more businesses had ramifications beyond the borders of a single state and were thus inappropriate for local regulation. The judges knew this and it was reflected, among other things, in their opinions.

But along with this knowledge there developed a complementary and to some extent transcendent feeling that government regulation in general was dangerously increasing and that the judiciary had a holy obligation to help avert the peril if it could. In the early stage the feeling could not be implemented via the Fourteenth Amendment, because judicial conscience did not permit an interpretation of the Amendment that was unwarranted by precedent. But in the commerce field, as we have noted, the precedent did exist, and the Court was inclined from the first to use the *Cooley* rule and related ideas against the regulatory threat. The fact that the decisions invoked the new realities of commercial nationalism was important; these realities added a significant weight to the balance, supplying a powerful argument and sometimes no doubt helping to change a judge's mind. But to suggest that considerations of nationalism were predominant is to confuse the postwar Court with its predecessors, to forget that the old issue of federalism was now becoming subordinate to the "higher" issue of economic control.

That subordination was made abundantly clear in the 1890's, when the Court was finally confronted with national regulatory statutes of major dimensions. Two cases in point are enough to illuminate the matter. After the *Wabash* decision, Congress finally bestirred itself to pass the act which established the Interstate Commerce Commission for regulating the railroads. The Commission's efforts were impeded from the outset by corporate opposition and court-contrived incumbrances. But the great blow fell in 1896 when the Supreme Court announced that the act did not endow the Commission with the power to fix railroad rates (*Cincinnati, New Orleans, and Texas Pacific Railway Co. v. I.C.C.*). As Justice Harlan remarked a year later, the Commission was now left with power "to make reports, and to issue protests. But it has been shorn, by judicial interpretation, of authority to do anything of an effective character."

The second illustrative case is equally edifying. It involved the Sherman Act, which had been passed by Congress in 1890 to "protect trade and commerce against unlawful restraints and monopolies." In 1895, the Court held that the law did not, and indeed could not, forbid monopolies in manufacturing, because manufacturing is not a part of interstate commerce and effects interstate commerce only "indirectly." To allow the national government to regulate this subject would be to permit encroachment on the reserved powers of the states (*United States v. E. C. Knight Co.*).

In the face of these decisions handcuffing national authority and in the face of the line of decisions already discussed which correspondingly restricted state control of commerce, it is a little hard to think of "nationalist" or "localist" considerations as dominant in the Court's value scale. The inescapable implication is, on the contrary, that the Court's chief concern was to defend the principle of laissez faire and that both nationalist and localist doctrine were being pressed to subserve that end. The minions of the "onward march of communism" would find no comfort in the commerce clause, if the Supreme Court could prevent it. And to an impressive degree the Court could.

THE NEW FOURTEENTH AMENDMENT: THE TRIUMPH
OF JUDICIAL CONSTITUTION-MAKING

However, if the battle of laissez faire was to be waged with effectiveness, some more potent weapon than the commerce clause was needed, for, versatile though that instrument was, it was not a universal answer to the individualist's prayers. Suppose a business falls clearly within the range of interstate or intrastate commerce; what is to save it then? Not the distinctions just discussed; they have been eliminated by definition. Yet unless some alternate doctrine can be discovered, the state and national governments will be left free to impose the most arbitrary restraints on business, and laissez faire will be, as far as constitutional limitations are concerned, a lost cause.

Precisely this point was made by counsel in *Munn* v. *Illinois*, the "Granger case" decided in 1877. Illinois and other western states had recently witnessed popular uprisings against the rate-fixing practices of the railroads and associated enterprises; the state law in question here set limits on the charges for grain storage in the Chicago area, but Illinois and her neighbors had also passed measures fixing maximum railroad rates, and conservative opinion had been deeply agitated by these assaults on free enterprise. Yet the lawyers who spoke for that element—specifically in this case for the grain elevators—were in rather the position of Mr. Campbell in *Slaughter-House:* their passionate conviction that the Constitution ought to prohibit these outrages was more impressive than their legal arguments that the Fourteenth Amendment had been designed to provide such a prohibition. Consequently, their arguments were heavily tinged with the idea that the Court had a moral duty to remake the Amendment into a bastion "behind which private rights and private property may shelter themselves and be safe" from "the will of the majority."

And this plea was meanwhile being echoed in the argument of other Granger cases before the Court, in speeches and legal periodicals, indeed almost everywhere the judges might turn, except of course in the "radical" press. The judiciary (and in fact America as a whole) were being deluged by a potpourri composed of Social Darwinist philosophy about the survival of the fittest and the virtues of economic freedom; scholarly appearing but largely irrelevant citations from the Anglo-American legal past; and admonitions that the judicial power alone had the means at its disposal to save the nation from suicide-by-regulation.

In the face of all this, it speaks well for the self-restraint of the Court that it rejected the immediate call to duty and upheld the Granger acts, including the grain elevator statute. Businesses like the present one, said Chief Justice Waite in the *Munn* case, are "affected with a public interest" because their owners have chosen to use their property "in a manner to make it of public consequence, and affect the community at large." When property is so used, its possessor must submit to public control, including rate regulation.

But the consternation of the proponents of laissez faire at this outcome demonstrates that they had not read the opinion carefully, or perhaps that, like so many critics of the Court in American history, they were more interested in an immediately favorable decision than in the long-term principle they had so fervently espoused. Had they read more attentively and thought more farsightedly, they must have seen that the majority's sales resistance was really weaker than a superficial reading might reveal, that their arguments had, after all, struck home. For Waite was careful to say that "under some circumstances" a regulatory statute might be so arbitrary as to be unconstitutional, and these mild words implied for the business community a concession whose value was beyond emeralds and rubies. It meant that the Court recognized, back-handedly to be sure but without question, that the due process clause of the Fourteenth Amendment imposed a substantive limit on economic legislation. Such an interpretation was too novel in 1877 to support an outright holding of unconstitutionality, but Waite had given the supplicants notice that their prayers were not unheeded, and also a kind of promissory note, redeemable when precedents had ripened a bit further and judicial backs had been stiffened a bit more.

The history of the Fourteenth Amendment for the remainder of the nineteenth century is one of gradual redemption of that promise made in 1877. But for some years the approach to the question was oblique, and the cumulative tendency of the decisions must have seemed equivocal to contemporaries. Instead of forthrightly invalidating a statute by applying a substantive view of due process, the judges chose to uphold the challenged laws, and concurrently to issue more or less explicit warnings that other laws in other circumstances might not be treated so tenderly. In 1886, for example, Waite allowed a Mississippi statute endowing a railroad commission with the power to fix rates, but he seized the occasion to remark that the Commission must beware of fixing charges so low that it might amount "to a taking of private property for public use without just compensation or without due process of law." If "due process" simply meant "due procedure," its historic connotation, the actual amount of the rates established was beyond judicial cognizance so long as the Commission observed procedural amenities like notice and hearing. Quite evidently Waite was assuming, though not for the moment employing, judicial power to restrain "injustice" if it should occur.

This assumption was a product, no doubt, of many converging factors: the multiplication of "welfare state" threats, the Macedonian cries of the business community and its legal and academic defenders, a growing awareness that an interpretation of due process which seemed impossibly novel and probably unnecessary a decade before could be made acceptable by slow accretion and might prove very useful in the cause of righteousness. As Waite wrote, the voices of two great contemporaries, Thomas M. Cooley and Stephen J. Field, must have been echoing in his mind. Cooley's classic treatise on *Constitutional Limitations,* first published in 1868, had become a canonical text for jurists, and his support of due process in its emerging form gave the stamp of scholarly approval to an interpretation that seemed ethically more and more imperative. Field had been from the start eager to embrace an interpretation that would protect freedom of contract; his dissents had been resounding in the supreme courtroom for years, and each term these organ tones must have seemed a little more compelling. Justice Harlan, perhaps the strongest-minded on the bench at the time except Field, was patently moved by the impact of all these gathering forces. In 1887, though upholding a Kansas prohibition law against due process attack, he remarked that the Court in evaluating such legislation is not bound by "mere forms," and continued:

If, therefore, a statute purporting to have been enacted to protect the public health, the public morals, or the public safety, has no real or substantial relation to those objects . . . it is the duty of the courts so to adjudge and thereby give effect to the Constitution.

By the 1890's the development signalized by such pronouncements had run its course, and the concept of due process as a judicially enforced bar to arbitrary economic legislation was ready for action. Judicial minds had been gradually accommodated to an idea that had long since found its place in their hearts; dicta such as those just cited had accumulated in sufficient numbers so that "precedents" for the new doctrine could be readily invoked to satisfy a lawyer-like conscience. In 1890, the Court overturned a Minnesota railroad commission law on the ground that it "deprived the company of its right to a judicial investigation, by due process of law" of the reasonableness of rates. This seemed to mean that rates fixed by law or by commissions acting under law were subject to approval of courts, and ultimately the Supreme Court. There yet remained a margin of vagueness at this point, though the judges were obviously edging closer to their historic goal. But at all events doubts were swept away five years later in *Smyth* v. *Ames,* which flatly held that the judiciary has the last word on the reasonableness of rates, and even went on to propound what a later jurist called a "mischievous formula" for determining them. In 1897 the concept of "liberty of contract," so dear to Herbert Spencer and other defenders of laissez faire, was used as the basis for invalidating a state law; the Court as B. F. Wright says, "simply wrote the dissenting opinions of Justices Swayne and Bradley in the *Slaughter-House Cases* into the Fourteenth Amendment."

This holding completed the process of constitution-making that had begun with the dissents in that case. Ten years before, the Court had conceded, rather offhandedly, that corporations were "persons" within the meaning of the Amendment, and that concession was now seen to be of epic importance and of incalculable value to the business community. Combined with the now accepted idea of due process as a substantive limit on "arbitrary" laws, it meant that business, whether incorporated or not, was no longer wholly at the mercy of the popular will.

The development just chronicled is beyond much question the classic example of "government by judiciary" in the United States, and it is worthwhile to pause for a moment to underline some of its features. In the first place, it is noteworthy that the Court did not proceed by a single bound to this new doctrine and the new role that it made possible. This was the course urged by Field and other cheerleaders, but the majority preferred to grope more deliberately through the tangled thicket of modern government, to plant the judicial feet more warily. Strong men like Field, with a tinge of dogmatism, play an important part in American constitutional history, but less positive types like Waite are often more interesting because the problem of evaluating them is more subtle, and they tend to exemplify more faithfully the actual nature of American constitutional history.

For Field the problem was fairly simple: here is the businessman whom any just-minded judge should be honored to defend; and here is the due process clause; why not use it for that benign purpose? But the majority of his colleagues saw cross-threads in the tapestry: the proposed doctrine was strange and ill supported by precedent or public acceptance; impetuous and untimely decisions to assume the task of supervision might trap the judiciary in an impossible role of its own contriving. They held back, and this reluctance to make radical departures, to generalize adventurously, is characteristic of the historical Court. But it is also characteristic that their negative opinions provided an escape, that their "no" was qualified by a "perhaps."

That "perhaps" could swell to a certainty in the fullness of time by a process so subtle and complex that not even the craftsmen themselves would be fully aware of what was happening, and in the end both they and their observers could feel that the doctrine they applied was a familiar, indeed an immemorial, rule of law. Justice could be served, but the illusion of a changeless constitution need not be abandoned. And all this was achieved because the Court realized, whether instinctively or analytically does not matter, that the ambiguity of its mandate is both its limitation and its opportunity.

If due process had emerged as a dogmatic "rule" in 1873, it might have saved some corporate profits for a while, but the pressures of the welfare state would have forced the Court to scuttle it before long. The mature doctrine that became explicit in the 1890's was a far more effective tool of judicial governance, not only because it was now more securely backed by use and wont, but because it was flexible enough to mean anything the judiciary wanted it to mean. The Court could now help shape social policy toward capitalism, yet respect the boundaries imposed by economic necessity and political possibility.

THE TOOLS OF JUDICIAL SUPERVISION

With the maturation of substantive due process in the closing years of the nineteenth century, the Supreme Court was at length adequately equipped to play a part in resolving the major issue of the era—that of business-government relationships. The new Fourteenth Amendment and the commerce clause doctrines earlier described made almost every governmental intervention in economic affairs the business of the judiciary, to approve or disapprove, as discretion might dictate. The Court had finally adjusted itself and the Constitution to the altered conditions of the postwar order. Old problems like slavery had been forgotten. The question of Negro rights and with it the question of civil rights in general, had been relegated to a minor and almost negligible place among the Court's concerns. The once preponderant issue of federalism was now subordinated to the government-business preoccupation: the formerly ruling value of nationalism was replaced by a judicial ideal called economic freedom. The process of redefining the Court's role, a process impelled by the transfiguration of the nation itself, was not complete to be sure. But the enabling conditions had been met; the judges had surmounted traditional interpretations which would have left them impotent to play any significant role at all. They now had the tools, so to speak, to do the job to which they felt they were summoned by their legacy and their consciences. How they would use those tools, what role they would actually assume, what result they would work for in arbitrating the business-government relationship—are questions for the next chapter.

VI

The Judiciary and the Welfare State:
1900–1937

In 1900 the Supreme Court's position is somewhat that of a medieval knight-bachelor on the morning after his accolade. The long novitiate as a squire has been served, the vigil has been kept, the rituals have been performed. The gilded spurs and the sword are ready, and the world is waiting. Will the chevalier at once launch an intrepid campaign to slay all the dragons of "socialism" and rescue all the maidens of "free enterprise"? Or will he exercise his hard-won rights and powers moderately, bearing in mind that there are differences in vulnerability even among dragons and that some maidens may be more virtuous than others and more worthy of chivalry's attentions?

These were the two clear-cut alternatives open to the Court, and for clarity's sake it would be gratifying to record that the judges elected one or the other. But the fact of the matter is a little more intricate. Instead of adopting either of these courses of action wholeheartedly, the Court established a kind of dialectic involving both of them and managed to live in this apparently uneasy state for the next thirty-odd years. Sometimes the judges talked in this period as if they were determined to halt the regulatory movement in its tracks and as if they had the will and power to veto any political impulse they disapproved. Yet at other times, and often even concurrently, they ratified many inroads on the free enterprise ideal and sought only to moderate, not to stop, the growth of government intervention.

Such judicial dualism is easy enough to understand. The first notion—that the Court could and should use its new armaments to arrest the drift toward regulation—had its origin partly in the deep sense of horror that words like "socialism" generated in judicial breasts, and partly in the rhetoric of judicial supremacy that had been accumulating for over a century. Marshall's assertion in *Marbury* that "there is no middle ground" between the idea of judicial control and the idea of unlimited government; the statement of Davis in *Milligan* that the Constitution "covers with the shield of its protection all classes of men, at all times, and under all circumstances"; Field's repeated contentions that the Court had the authority and duty to defend "inalienable rights, rights which are the gift of the Creator" against all comers—such words had a certain impact on the minds of the judges themselves as well as of their auditors. The priesthood more than half believed the mythology it had helped to create; and the impulse to monarchize and kill with looks was therefore very strong.

But the same judges were at the same time more or less dimly aware of certain other factors and shared certain other attributes. Most of them had played some part in practical affairs, and their hostility to regulation in general was tempered by the realization that particular circumstances cannot always be governed by dogmatism. Moreover, the record of judicial history on which they drew was replete not only with mythic incantations like those of Marshall, Davis, and Field, but also with concrete examples of judicial forbearance. In a word, the Court of the past had often talked in absolutist terms, but had usually acted discreetly and flexibly. And the judges of the twentieth century were thus torn between the rhetorical and the historic forms of the judicial image. In general they used the veto power inherent in such doctrines as commerce and due process far more selectively and judiciously than the fierce champions of laissez faire would have preferred. The vision of judicial tyranny that emerges from some of the critical literature of the 1920's and 1930's, the picture of a great nation shackled helplessly by judge-made law, is pretty remote from the fact. Even in the heyday of judicial negativism, the affirmative note was also frequently sounding; many of the most notable negative decisions turned out upon close examination to be less absolutist than they at first appeared.

Yet neither can it be denied that the judges seemed recurrently tempted during these years to have done with temporizing, to attack with their bright new weapons, to rule by flat decree. This impulse emerged most often in dissenting opinions where language was least likely to be qualified by considerations of responsibility; it showed itself in an occasional majority decision during the first three decades, in cases which peculiarly outraged judicial sensibilities. Evidently there was a certain tension between the desire to influence and the desire to rule. In general, the chevalier conducted himself with reasonable modesty and decorum. But always in the background was the fond idea that a really intrepid assault might dispose of the dragons and that a world without them would be a pleasant place. Throughout the period there was a constant under-current of threat that the rhetorical could become the actual, if the provocation were great enough.

THE POWER TO TAX AND JUDICIAL SUBJECTIVISM

As the judges of the Supreme Court looked about them in the closing years of the nineteenth century and the early years of the twentieth, they could see threats to free enterprise rearing up on every side in numbers that seemed to increase year by year. They had rejected, as we have seen, the politically im-possible plea of Mr. Campbell in the *Slaughter-House Cases* to establish a wall against all such invasions; and they were now faced with the nice task of distinguishing between interlopers that were tolerable and others that were not. Their moral in-stincts might be thought a sufficient guide by some, but what was needed was a legal rule, and it is hard to translate a moral instinct into a legal rule without losing something in the transla-tion. The judges yearned for a formula, or set of them, which would objectively discriminate between permissible and im-permissible economic statutes. If they acted merely in terms of a subjective ethic, they exposed themselves to the suggestion that perhaps the next man's ethic was as good as their own.

The power of taxation illustrates these problems with special force, for the power can be used, unless somehow checked, to accomplish prodigies of public control; yet it is peculiarly hard to formulate a rule that will limit it reasonably. And the Con-stitution provides little help; the clauses relating to taxation are few and hardly self-explanatory. It is not surprising, as the clamor for social justice grew, that the tax power was called upon to right wrongs, as well as to fill the public treasury.

From the point of view of the businessman, the most horrendous of these forays against capital was the federal income tax law, passed in 1894, which exempted incomes up to $4,000 and imposed a levy of 2 per cent above that amount. The law had been squeezed through Congress only after years of agitation; it was frankly an attempt to tax the well-to-do; and it seemed to many as it did to Justice Field "but the beginning" of "a war of poor against the rich" which would threaten the foundations of the Republic. Certainly it would at any rate deplete the pocketbooks of a good many solid citizens, and a constitutional challenge was rushed to the courts. It was argued among other things that the tax was invalid as applied to the income from real estate (that is, rents) and from personal property, because these were "direct taxes" and must be apportioned among the states in accordance with their population (Art. I, sec. 2). Apportionment by population would of course kill the principle of apportionment on the basis of ability to pay, which was the major concern of those who had passed the law.

But the challengers faced the apparently grave difficulty that the Court had, in 1881, unanimously upheld the income tax that had been levied during and immediately after the Civil War; and their case was further undermined in advance by the ancient *Hylton* decision of 1796, in which it had been intimated that only "head taxes" and real estate taxes were "direct" within the meaning of the Constitution and thus subject to the apportionment requirement. Their glittering array of high-priced counsel, including such ornaments of the contemporary bar as George F. Edmunds and Joseph Choate, was therefore forced to argue that the Court should reverse "a century of error" in order to stop the "communistic march." Five members of the Court were ultimately persuaded, after elaborate argument and reargument, that this was indeed their duty, and the income tax law was scuttled by judicial fiat. The direct tax clause, so long neglected as a constitutional restraint, provided the judges with an objective formulation of their prejudice in favor of wealth. It is a kind of anticlimax that the enactment of the Sixteenth Amendment in 1913 deprived them of this self-created mooring post. It declared that Congress could, without apportionment, tax incomes "from whatever source derived" and most of the nice distinctions of the Income Tax decision came tumbling down; capital was again exposed to the communistic threat from which Choate and the Court had temporarily rescued it.

One of those distinctions, however, had long antedated 1895 and was destined to survive for many years thereafter. Among the vices of the income tax had been the fact that it applied to income from municipal bonds. It was thus, the Court had said, a tax upon the powers and instrumentalities of the state, and such intergovernmental taxation is forbidden by the principles of the federal system. This doctrine derived originally from Marshall's pronouncement in *McCulloch* v. *Maryland* (1819) that "the power to tax involves the power to destroy." It followed, thought Marshall's successors, that neither the state nor the national government could tax the other's instrumentalities, for the Constitution supposes the independent existence of both governments, and to allow such taxes would be to allow the taxing government to destroy the taxed government.

With the aid of such reasoning the Court had woven a complex web of reciprocal tax immunities, and it would be more wearisome than profitable to explore them in detail. It might be thought that the Sixteenth Amendment, empowering the federal government to tax incomes without apportionment "from whatever source derived," had relieved Congress of worries about taxing the income of state employees (whose offices had been held many years before to be state instrumentalities and thus exempt from federal taxation). But the Supreme Court ruled otherwise. From the point of view of this volume perhaps the chief significance of this whole doctrine is the light it sheds on the Court's prevailing habit of mind—the idea that government cannot be left judicially unsupervised in possession of a power that *might* be abused. It was suggested from time to time that it would be soon enough to worry when one government actually did seek to destroy or burden another by taxing its instrumentalities unreasonably, and that meanwhile the judiciary should leave the tax policy alone. But the Court of the twentieth century was not disposed to lift its hand from the reins even so conditionally.

Still another problem raised by taxation was presented when the taxing power was used to accomplish regulatory purposes. Such laws of course might endanger the sacrosanct principle of laissez faire, and some restraint on them was, therefore, evidently desirable, but how to frame such a restraint without frankly admitting that the Court was simply second-guessing the legislature on a question of social policy?

The difficulty is illustrated when we compare *McCray* v. *United States* in 1904, with the Child Labor Tax Case in 1922. In the former, the Court upheld a federal law imposing a heavy tax on oleomargarine colored to resemble butter, the obvious effect and purpose of the tax being to discourage manufacture of the product. The Court, said Justice White, cannot condemn an otherwise valid tax because it objects to the motives that prompted the law's passage, for those motives are not within the scope of proper judicial inquiry. This seemed to mean that regulatory results could be achieved by taxation without fear of court interference, a doctrine that would create vast opportunities for control. However, in later cases the Court began to hint that regulatory taxes might be subject to scrutiny if the provisions for collecting them were not clearly related to the gathering of revenue, and in the Child Labor Tax Case these hints were confirmed. Congress had laid a tax of 10 per cent on the profits of production industries that employed children, obviously banking on the assumption that the regulatory purpose of the tax would be beyond judicial cognizance. But, said the Court, "there comes a time in the extension of the penalizing features of the so-called tax when it loses its character as such and becomes a mere penalty with the characteristics of regulation and punishment. Such is the case in the law before us." The difference between this law and the law in the *McCray* case is that the purpose to control child labor is evident *on the law's face;* the purpose to inhibit manufacture and sale of colored margarine was not similarly evident.

But the trouble is that it *was*. Plainly the Court's ruling in the later case was prompted by the feeling that control over child labor was not and should not be vested in the national government, just as its ruling in *McCray* was explained by the feeling among the judiciary that it did no great harm to restrict the production of colored margarine. As judgments of social policy either of these pronouncements might be open to argument, but at least the argument would be relevant. The Court's difficulty was that it must try to cloak the social judgments in the form of constitutional rules, and the attempt was ultimately unavailing. A flat rule that the motivations of a tax could not be scrutinized would clarify the constitutional process, but it would allow governmental interference in fields which the judges thought best left free from interference. The alternative was the doctrine that the tax would be disallowed if its regulatory purpose was evident "on its face," and this reintroduced the subjective factor in judicial decision-making. For whether the judge finds an intent to penalize on the face of the law is likely to depend on whether he smiles or frowns on the purpose of the penalty. As so often in the cases of this era, the Court had been unable to develop an objective formula that would distinguish between acceptable and unacceptable departures from the free enterprise ideal. By their ultimate resort to subjectivism, the judges kept their hands on the reins and retained their freedom of discretion. But they made it harder to convince observers that judicial review was more than another step in the legislative process.

NEW CHECK-REINS ON THE COMMERCE POWER

This subjectivism of judicial control, evident enough in the tax field, becomes even plainer when we examine the Court's decisions involving interstate commerce. The judicial problem here was especially difficult to cope with though it is comparatively easy to state. The commerce clause is a grant of power to the national government, and the pre–Civil War courts had uniformly interpreted that power broadly. Unless such affirmative interpretations are qualified, they make it possible for national statutes to regulate the national economy unmercifully, and the battle for constitutional laissez faire is lost in advance. Negative formulas must, therefore, be devised, and in the

E. C. Knight case of 1895, as we have seen, the Court answered this challenge by forbidding federal control of manufacturing on the ground that Congress may regulate only interstate commerce itself and that which affects interstate commerce "directly."

Another potent array of negativisms was assembled in *Hammer* v. *Dagenhart* in 1918. Spurred by the same reformers who were later to bring about the passage of the Child Labor Tax discussed in the preceding section, Congress had forbidden the passage through interstate commerce of products manufactured by firms that employed children. Under the *Knight* doctrines Congress could not directly forbid child labor, for the control of production was vested exclusively in the states; but the legislators evidently assumed that they could strike at the product of such labor *after* it entered interstate commerce, for they had often been told that Congress' power over that commerce was plenary. In fact the Supreme Court had previously upheld national laws that seemed clearly analogous, such as the Mann Act, which barred prostitutes from interstate commerce, and the Pure Food and Drug Act, which barred adulterated food.

The hearts of the judges were troubled, however. If Congress could exclude from interstate commerce any article it chose to exclude, then it could in effect control production, for most firms were dependent upon interstate commerce for their market. Therefore, the Court in a triumphantly negative mood announced that the power to prohibit goods from moving through interstate commerce was subject to limitations previously unknown. Congress could bar such goods if their transportation was followed by "harmful results" (for example, immorality in the case of prostitutes, ptomaine poisoning in the case of adulterated foods). But since the evil aimed at here, child labor, occurs *before* interstate commerce begins, and since the product transported (for example, a can of shrimp) is in itself harmless, the law must fall. The act is repugnant to the Constitution "in a twofold sense."

It not only transcends the authority delegated to Congress over commerce but also exerts a power as to a purely local matter to which the federal authority cannot extend. . . . if Congress can thus regulate matters entrusted to local authority . . . the power of the States over local matters may be eliminated, and thus our system of government be practically destroyed.

Here then, it might be thought, was a whole set of criteria, of legal rules, that could be used by the Court to mitigate the headlong advance toward public control of the nation's economy. But there was a fly or two in the ointment. For one thing, it was becoming increasingly apparent to those of even modest political sensitivity that the public demand for some form of economic regulation was rising and could not be altogether gainsaid. The first decade of the twentieth century had witnessed after all "the progressive era"; the revelations of the muckrakers had stirred the popular consciousness; one president had publicly chided "the malefactors of great wealth" and another had spoken eloquently about "the new freedom." For another thing, as has been suggested earlier, the members of the Court were not simple obstructionists. Most of them were flexible enough to realize that Herbert Spencer's ideal order was not literally attainable, that in some circumstances government interference with economic activity could serve a useful end. And the case for such interference was likely to seem especially strong when the challenged statute was designed to protect and promote commerce rather than to shackle it, or was designed to stamp out evils that the judges themselves regarded as objectionable, morally or otherwise.

The Judiciary and the Welfare State

As a consequence of such considerations, the Court proceeded to qualify and attenuate the negative doctrines of the *Knight* and *Dagenhart* cases in a long series of decisions that exude a quite different spirit. But it is both characteristic and significant that these affirmative doctrines were created, not to replace the negativisms just described, but to exist side by side with them as alternative formulations.

This process is illustrated in two fields involving two of the most awesome problems of modern American industrial society —the trusts and the railroads. It will be remembered that the *Knight* decision had gravely crippled the Sherman Antitrust Act, since it amounted to a judicial veto of the program to control the trusts. Within a very few years, however, the judges began to have second thoughts, and they upheld antitrust proceedings in a number of decisions that seemed to reflect a mood of tolerance toward the necessities of government control. The sharp distinction of the *Knight* case between local and national affairs had indeed the merit of clarity, but it had the defect of impracticality. It made no sense to insist that an activity was "local" in character when its effects were unquestionably national; a tidal wave may originate in mid-ocean yet flood the shores of New York.

These realities were trenchantly acknowledged by Justice Holmes in 1905 in a case involving prosecution of the "beef trust." The packers had conspired to control the sale of meat in Chicago, which was of course the "hog butcher of the world." These sales agreements were evidently as local as the manufacturing agreements of the *Knight* case, but the Court's approach to them was very different:

Commerce among the States is not a technical legal conception, but a practical one, drawn from the course of business. When cattle are sent for sale from a place in one state, with the expectation that they will end their transit, after purchase, in another, and when in effect they do so, with only the interruption necessary to find a purchaser at the stock yards, and when this is a typical, constantly recurring course, the current thus existing is a current of commerce among the states, and that purchase of the cattle is a part and incident of such commerce.

In short, the whole "stream of commerce" including sales is subject to federal control; the Court, as Chief Justice Taft was to remark in a later case, would not frustrate antitrust policy by indulging in a "nice and technical inquiry" to distinguish between the local and the national. Indeed it was precisely such a "nice and technical" excursion which the Court had allowed itself in the *Knight* case, but a petty consistency, as Emerson said, is the hobgoblin of little minds.

As for federal railroad regulation, the Court here displayed an acquiescent temper that was often shocking to the proponents of laissez faire and is most difficult to reconcile with the dogmatisms of the *Knight* and *Dagenhart* decisions. The statutory interpretations of the 1890's had shorn the Interstate Commerce Commission of effective power, but Congress duly repaired the damage, endowing the Commission with ample authority, including control over rates. It might be expected that the Court would greet these developments coldly and would assail them with all the resources of the constitutional armory. But in fact the judges cheerfully upheld the laws and approved Commission orders that deeply impaired the supposedly sacred reserved powers of the states.

Perhaps the high point of such judicial toleration was reached in the *Dayton–Goose Creek Railway* case of 1924, which upheld the Transportation Act of 1920. This law required railroads which earned more than a certain fixed "fair return" to turn over one-half of the excess to the Commission and to hold the rest in a reserve fund to be used as the Commission directed. Even worse, the requirement applied to income earned on wholly intrastate business. But the provisions gave the Court no constitutional qualms. The power to regulate commerce, said Chief Justice Taft for a unanimous Court, is a power "to foster, protect and control the commerce with appropriate regard to the welfare of those who are immediately concerned, as well as the public at large, and to promote its growth and insure its safety." In exercising this wide authority over interstate affairs, Congress may also control intrastate commerce, if state and interstate operations are "inextricably commingled." In short, the whole national railway system is subject to federal control, and the "nice and technical" distinctions based on the Tenth Amendment have little or no bearing in this field.

The contrast between the *Knight* and *Dagenhart* doctrines on the one hand and these antitrust and railway doctrines on the other would be bewildering if it were not for the hint the Chief Justice drops in the words just quoted. Congress, he tells us, may "foster, protect and control" commerce to its heart's content; that is, it may do things that are "good" for commerce, but not (so the implication runs) things that are "bad" for it. This point is comparable to the one made in the *Dagenhart* case: that the law can bar "bad" things from interstate commerce, but not "good" things. The translation of both dicta is this: that the Constitution forbids those departures from laissez faire that the Court disapproves, and permits those departures that the Court thinks reasonable and proper. And obviously this is not a legal "rule" in any understandable sense of the word, but a statement of social policy, or rather an assertion of the power to determine it. Under these loose standards the Court can either uphold or overthrow almost any commercial regulation it encounters, depending on whether the judges approve or disapprove the economic policy the law represents. The advantage of this arrangement is that it enables the Court to choose discreetly the dragons it will fight and the maidens it will rescue. But the disadvantage, as in the tax cases, is that it becomes harder and harder to sustain the illusion that the judicial yes or no is based on inexorable constitutional commands, and it becomes easier and easier for observers to see that judicial review is operating as a subjective and quasi-legislative process.

DUE PROCESS AND THE COURT'S REARGUARD ACTION

In the tax cases and in the commerce cases, as we have seen, the Supreme Court had conducted only occasional and rather limited forays against the welfare state. America had been notified that there were limits on these two great powers, and this in itself was important, for it preserved the idea of judicial sovereignty, and the knowledge that the Court was keeping an eye on things might discourage some socialistic ventures before their start. But the actual negative decisions of importance were few, and the march toward regulation had been at most deflected slightly and, here and there, somewhat delayed. However, the sharpest weapon in the judicial panoply, as the last chapter suggested, was the due process clause. That clause was available as a limit on both federal and state government. In its modern form it allowed the Court to reach not only procedural but also substantive questions. If the Court was to control American economic policy in any significant way, due process was obviously its major resource.

The Judiciary and the Welfare State

The feats that were accomplished with this clause in the 1900–1937 period are by no means unimpressive. B. F. Wright has counted some 184 decisions between 1899 and 1937 which invalidated state laws on the basis of either the due process or equal protection clause (the two were frequently used by the judiciary in tandem; it is often, though not invariably, true that a denial of equal protection is also regarded as a denial of due process). Those involving federal laws were far fewer. But according to accepted doctrine, the term "due process" has the same meaning in both the Fifth and Fourteenth Amendments, and it follows that the prohibitions announced against state action were usually presumptively applicable to national laws as well, if Congress might venture to enact them. There is no way of estimating reliably the restraining effect of this cloud of negativisms on state legislators and congressmen who might otherwise have made haste more speedily along the road to the welfare state. No doubt the pace of social change was moderated; a respectable number of "excesses" were prevented; a respectable amount of money was saved for the businessman; a good many laborers were left a little hungrier than they might have been if the Court had not been there to defend economic liberty.

Yet it is highly questionable that the due process clause was a major factor in determining the drift of American economic policy during this period. Most of the important legislative measures that were really demanded by public opinion did pass and did manage to survive the gauntlet of judicial review. In some conspicuous areas, like maximum hours legislation, the Court fought a delaying action for a few years and then, when the trend of public demand became unmistakable, gave in. In only a few instances was its position really adamant, and even here the restraining effect of judicial pronouncements is conjectural. Laws are not automatically invalidated because they happen to conflict logically with the doctrine of a previous Supreme Court decision; a case must be brought against each one, and that case must often be carried through extensive labyrinths of the judicial system for years before the law can be pronounced technically dead. Because of such circumstances a great mass of regulatory legislation survived untouched even in these halcyon days of due process. The fact that there was not more such legislation, the fact that Americans during the 1920's tolerated so great a measure of social injustice—this is to be attributed to public apathy amounting to callousness, not to the Supreme Court. To be sure, the Court did its bit to generate and encourage that public mood. But this is very different from saying that the Court rather than the nation was primarily responsible for the failures of public policy.

The virtue of the modern concept of due process was its remarkable flexibility. It allowed the Court to invalidate any law that struck a majority of the members as "arbitrary" or "capricious." These wonderfully ambiguous definitions brought practically the whole world of regulatory legislation within the potential reach of a judicial veto. But, even better, their ambiguity permitted the judiciary to exercise or withhold that veto in any given case, subject to no guiding principles except the judges' own sense of discretion.

The network of "ayes" and "nays" that they fashioned with the help of this carte blanche is too complex for brief summary. A great variety of regulatory measures were scrutinized. Tax laws were queried and sometimes overthrown on the ground that the state had no "jurisdiction to tax" the source in question, or simply on the ground that the tax was arbitrarily administered. State legislation regulating the weight of loaves of bread, prohibiting the use of "shoddy" in quilts, requiring a railroad to construct an underpass for a farmer's personal convenience, were held to deny due process or equal protection of the laws.

But perhaps the most important and instructive pattern of judicial intervention was developed in connection with the problem of rates—prices and wages. And there is a special significance in this field from the judicial point of view, because rates for goods sold or services performed are the very keystone of the free enterprise system. Any state interference with them impinges vitally on freedom of contract, which is the holy of holies for the knights-errant of laissez faire. It might well be expected that the Court would look hard at legislative innovation in this field.

In *Lochner* v. *New York* (1905) this expectation was amply fulfilled. The case concerned working hours rather than wages, but as Chief Justice Taft was later to say, the one is the multiplier and the other the multiplicand, and the operative point for the Court was that the state was seeking to control the heart of the working contract. The law restricted the hours of bakers in New York to ten per day or sixty per week. To Justice Peckham and the majority, this presented a grave challenge to the principle of contractual freedom, for if bakers' hours could be regulated, then so, presumably, could the hours of all other workers. The Court was prepared to concede that working hours in particularly dangerous occupations could be controlled in order to protect the workers' health. Or it would allow hours regulation if it could be shown that long hours might adversely affect the health of the public at large (for example, by leading to the production of unhealthful bread).

But neither of these statements can be made about the baking trade, which is not perhaps "absolutely and perfectly healthy" but is "vastly more healthy than [certain] others." To permit its regulation then would expose all or most occupations to hours regulation, would subject the working contract to "the mercy of legislative majorities." The police power cannot be allowed to reach so far; the law is an example of "meddlesome interferences with the rights of the individual," and it violates due process.

The *Lochner* decision represents one of those moments in the Court's twentieth-century history when the judges temporarily embraced the illusion that the regulatory movement could be halted, rather than merely delayed, by judicial pronouncement. The exceptions they allow to the rule against hours laws—the particularly unhealthy occupation principle—should not obscure the fact that a hard line has been drawn. Hereafter, if constitutional limits are as immutable as the mythology attests, American workmen shall be generally free from restraints on their right to work a twelve-hour day. Departures from the model of Herbert Spencer's *Social Statics* will be permitted up to a point, but at that point they must stop.

But in the actual event the process of judicial governance did not work that way. It seldom has. Justice Holmes, filing one of his earliest and most powerful dissents in this case, said:

I think that the word liberty in the Fourteenth Amendment is perverted when it is held to prevent the natural outcome of a dominant opinion unless it can be said that a rational and fair man necessarily would admit that the statute proposed would infringe fundamental principles as they have been understood by the traditions of our people and our law. It does not need research to show that no such sweeping condemnation can be passed upon the statute before us.

The majority opinion had stated, or implied, that "dominant opinion" does not matter, that the criterion of constitutionality is not traditional fundamental principles, but the individual conscience of the judge, and that a flat rule against general hours regulation was now laid down. However, when we follow the course of doctrine through the next twenty years, we find that it often runs closer to Holmes' standards than the judges themselves may have realized. Or perhaps it would be more accurate to say that it alternates between Peckham's uncompromising defense of free enterprise and Holmes' extreme permissiveness, with the balance of decisions on the latter side.

Three years after *Lochner* the Court found an exception to the flat rule of that case when faced by a statute regulating the hours of females. The social and physical characteristics of women, said the Court, put them at a special disadvantage in the struggle for subsistence, and it is therefore reasonable for the state to limit the hours they can be worked. And in 1917, a new majority took leave of the *Lochner* doctrine altogether, upholding an hours law for manufacturing establishments as a health measure (*Bunting* v. *Oregon*). The startling thing about this opinion by Justice McKenna was that it seemed to assume the validity of hours regulation and focused most of the argument on an answer to the charge that the law sought to regulate *wages* indirectly. *Lochner* was not even mentioned, though counsel had invoked it repeatedly in the briefs. Plainly the Court was showing itself more sensitive to "dominant opinions" than the pristine view of judicial sovereignty would allow. Yet it should not be thought that the Court was giving up contractual freedom entirely to "the mercy of legislative majorities." Only two years before, the judges had affirmed that the state could not, in order to equalize the parties engaged in collective bargaining, outlaw "yellow dog" contracts (agreements, as a condition of employment, that an employee will not join a labor union). Even in *Bunting* there was a hint that the wage contract was still sacrosanct, though hours regulations were not. The Court had taken advantage of the flexibility of due process to yield an outpost or two; for the moment the counsel of modesty and discretion had prevailed. But the *Lochner* spirit of hostility to social change, the *Lochner* illusion of judicial omnipotence, were not dead; they only slept. And a new majority, confronted by new threats to the wage-price nexus, might at any time call them to action again.

A rather similar pattern of judicial outlook and behavior can be traced in the cases involving the doctrine of "business affected with a public interest." This doctrine, it will be remembered, enjoyed its modern rebirth in *Munn* v. *Illinois*, in which Waite had used it to distinguish between rate regulations that would violate due process and those that would not. A business affected with a public interest or "devoted to a public use" was subject to rate regulation. This emphatically did not mean that the state could impose such rates as whimsy dictated; and after 1895 the Court records are dotted with decisions holding that the rates prescribed for a railroad or other public utility were unreasonably low. But if a business could be judicially classified as falling within the rubric of "public interest," its rates could be subjected to some measure of government control.

The problem, of course, was what criteria to use in making such a classification. One possibility would be to adopt the common-sense idea that any business important to the public was "affected with a public interest." But this would legitimize rate regulation on a vast scale, and rates were so crucial to the capitalist system as the judges understood it that they could not in conscience make so unqualified a concession. (Compare their reluctance in *Lochner* to accede to a similarly general ratification of hours regulation.) Yet as the complexities of commercial life multiplied in the twentieth century, it became evident even to conservative judges that there were many businesses whose prices could not be allowed to run wild.

The judicial solution was to allow rate regulation of a variety of businesses under the public interest principle, but to avoid commitment on the question of just what the principle meant, and thus to retain a potential veto. Franchise industries (those enjoying special, government-granted privileges) and public service industries like railroads and electric power companies, clearly fell within the charmed circle. So did certain traditionally regulated occupations like hotel-keeping and taxicab service. Finally, as Chief Justice Taft was to explain, there is another group of industries which have come to be public because "the owner, by devoting his business to the public use, in effect grants the public an interest in that use and subjects himself to public regulation. . . ." The Court so classified, for example, the business of fire insurance and the business of renting real estate in the District of Columbia during the war-engendered emergency. In fact, before 1923, the doctrine of public interest was never used restrictively, to hamper the development of the regulatory movement. But the rhetoric itself implied the possibility of restriction; the Court in making its concessions had been careful not to rule that possibility out. The affirmations of the past in this field were no more binding on the future than the acceptance of hours legislation in *Bunting* was a guaranty against judicial concern for the labor contract.

The American Supreme Court

With the advent of the 1920's the tone of judicial decisions, especially under the due process clause, was subtly altered. We have seen that the modern Court had developed in this area, as in others, an elaborate set of both negative and affirmative doctrines, thus establishing for the judiciary what Benjamin Cardozo called "the sovereign prerogative of choice." And we have further seen that the Court had so far been disposed to wield that prerogative discreetly, upholding many regulatory and welfare measures and using the veto more as a salutary threat than an instrument of continuous control.

In the 1920–29 period the number of negative decisions under the Fourteenth Amendment was almost double the number in the preceding decade. These figures themselves suggest some change in the constitutional climate, and the suggestion is confirmed by examination of individual decisions. True, a great many economic statutes still survived the judicial ordeal; prudent self-restraint was still an important Court theme. But the temper of the times, signalized by conservative Republican electoral triumphs and by the withering of the progressive spirit in public policy, was infectious. The spread of the infection was made somewhat more likely by the coming of men like Taft, Sutherland, and Butler to the bench, for all of them were deeply convinced foes of the welfare state. Now the judges were more confident that they spoke for the nation when they defended laissez faire. And the tension between modesty and boldness became greater; the illusion that the judiciary could really govern became a little more obtrusive, was reflected a little more often in actual decisions rather than mere rhetoric.

The Judiciary and the Welfare State

The spirit of the *Lochner* case, with its jealous concern for the sanctity of the labor contract, revived impressively in *Adkins* v. *Children's Hospital* (1923). Congress had established a board authorized to prescribe minimum wages for women and minors in the District of Columbia. The approval by the Court of hours regulation in *Bunting*, and of the Adamson Act (which controlled both wages and hours in the railroad industry in the war emergency) in a 1916 decision, had nourished reformist hopes that wage control would now be upheld. But the Court had carefully confined itself in those two opinions to the particular situation presented, and the implied reservations were now invoked. Justice Sutherland declared for the majority that the regulatory movement had once again gone too far. His opinion is an extremely able statement of the argument that minimum wage laws are unjust, mainly because they impose on the employer the burden to support partially indigent persons. This burden, he tells us, "if it belongs to anybody, belongs to society as a whole." Furthermore the statute is faulty in that the standard it sets for the board's guidance is impossibly vague. The board is required to set wages that will maintain the woman worker in good health and protect her morals. But no general wage standard can accomplish reliably the first aim for any particular person, because particular circumstances may vary. For example, "to those who practice economy, a given sum will afford comfort, while to those of contrary habit the same sum will be wholly inadequate." As for morals, "it cannot be shown that well paid women safeguard their morals more carefully than those who are poorly paid." Though liberty of contract is not absolute, it is "the general rule and restraint the exception." For the reasons given, the exception embodied in this law overpasses the limits of state power, and it is "the plain duty of the courts in the proper exercise of their authority to so declare."

Here again, then, as in *Lochner*, the Court had chosen a milepost on the road to the welfare state and elected to make a stand; here again was the idea that the judiciary could and should decide by flat decree great issues of economic control. Justice Sutherland's opinion was memorable because it reflected in classic form both the free enterprise position (exemplified in some of the gems just quoted) and the uncompromising conception of judicial authority and duty that never seems quite to die. And as the 1920's proceeded, the reminders that this conception was viable became more frequent.

It is particularly appropriate that that decade saw the negative threats of the public interest doctrine develop into realities. Chief Justice Taft used it in 1923 against a Kansas law that empowered a court of industrial relations to fix wages in the meat-packing industry, among others. Without deciding whether the meat-packing business was affected with a public interest in any sense, the Chief Justice held that it was not so *much* affected as to warrant wage-fixing. At this point the now mature and no longer innocuous doctrine was tendered into the care of Justice Sutherland who produced, in 1927, 1928, and 1932, three Court opinions that developed the negative implications most thoroughly. Theater ticket brokers, employment agencies, and ice companies were all excluded from the magic circle, which meant that their rates could not be publicly controlled and that certain other regulations which the Court regarded as excessive were likewise forbidden.

It became plain as the decisions proceeded that their effect was to protect all the "common callings" (the grocer, the dairyman, the butcher) from the peril of public rate control, and this interpretation, if adhered to, would indeed have been a significant restraint on the regulatory movement. But Sutherland's zeal for free enterprise and his absolutist approach to judicial duty were a trifle too extreme for his brethren. These unqualified rulings under the public interest doctrine had the effect of narrowing the range of judicial discretion, and the instinct for a more flexible standard asserted itself at last. In 1934, in *Nebbia* v. *New York,* the Court upheld a state law fixing minimum and maximum prices for milk, and took the occasion to announce that "there is no closed category of businesses affected with a public interest." The cherished idea that "there is something peculiarly sacrosanct" about prices was shattered by this announcement, and the Court's freedom of action in this field was restored. And simultaneously, of course, another obstacle in the path of the regulatory movement was cleared away.

THE JUDICIAL CHALLENGE TO THE NEW DEAL

The Supreme Court now stood, in 1934, at one of the great crossroads of its history. In the latter part of the nineteenth century it had built up, laboriously and piece by piece, a set of doctrines that could be employed for judicial supervision of the business-government relationship. By 1900 or thereabouts the doctrines were ready for service, but their existence did not settle the question of how the Court would employ them. Economic measures were now subject to judicial supervision, but the supervision could be strict and constant or lax and occasional, as the bench preferred. This freedom of choice was inherent in the tax doctrines, in the commerce doctrines, and above all in the due process doctrines that have been described.

The Court could use them to govern marginally, to moderate the pace of social reform, to force the nation to take a second look at extreme programs. It could, in short, operate as one influential factor among others in the process of social decision-making. Or it could alternatively seek to decide all the great political-economic questions that faced America, to halt the trend toward government intervention, to use its veto absolutely rather than suspensively.

The majority of the cases of the twentieth century through 1934 seem to reflect, as has been suggested, the former, modest approach. And this approach, for better or for worse, is surely the one most congruous with the Court's past history and most consistent with the conditions and limitations that were imposed on the judicial power by the peculiar circumstances of its origin in the United States. But a modest stance is often hard to maintain, perhaps especially in a democracy, and even more especially when myth and rhetoric encourage illusions of grandeur. So from time to time during these years, we find the other, monarchical vision emerging in a resounding decision, like *Dagenhart* or *Lochner* or *Adkins,* and we can observe this attractive self-image becoming stronger in the 1920's as forceful personalities like Sutherland speak for it in bold tones. In 1934, the Court seems balanced almost perfectly between these two conceptions of its role. With the elaborately varied precedents at the judges' disposal, they can swing either way. The regulatory trend that began so long ago in post–Civil War years has culminated in the New Deal; the welfare state, which Field and Cooley and Choate dreaded, seems at hand. The judiciary is bound to respond to it somehow, because for seventy years the judges have been sedulously cultivating the idea that the business-government relationship is, in part, at least, a judicial responsibility. The only question is which form the response will take.

For a time the issue hung in doubt, and there was even reason to believe that the Court would call upon its affirmative precedents, uphold national and state New Dealish innovations, and thus maintain a position on the margin of the political arena. After all, America was now beset by the gravest economic depression in her history, an emergency, as Justice Brandeis had remarked, "more serious than war." The decisions of the past three decades which had presumed to thwart economic legislation had been subjected to trenchant scholarly criticism, and the critics, such as Frankfurter, Corwin, and Powell, had been at pains to dispel the myth that the judges were mere agents of the Constitution, bound by its inexorable commands. Indeed the judges themselves had done their part to discredit that myth by insisting upon doctrinal flexibility in all the major areas of judicial control, by eschewing the objective rule. Most important of all perhaps, the New Deal was at this time enjoying a kind of honeymoon. The swift, decisive actions taken by Congress in the early days of Franklin Roosevelt's leadership were startling, but they seemed, to many at least, an improvement on the policy of stark inaction that had preceded them, and it was some time before doubts, even among the business community, were hardened into staunch opposition. The Supreme Court, despite protestations to the contrary, has seldom been insensitive to such considerations.

The *Nebbia* decision of 1934 had strongly suggested an acquiescent judicial temper. In the same year, the Court sustained a Minnesota law allowing courts to postpone mortgage foreclosures during the economic emergency. The law seemed to impair the obligation of contract, but Chief Justice Hughes held for a five-man majority that, in view of the emergency, some restraint on the enforcement of contractual rights was reasonable. The idea appeared to be that the states could now violate the contract clause so long as they were "reasonable" about it, and the existence of an emergency would be recognized as reflecting on the judgment of reasonableness. It is not surprising that the exponents of economic reform legislation began to hope for judicial approval of their programs. If the Court was willing to ratify departures in a field like the contract clause, where orthodoxy was fairly well defined, then the commerce clause, the tax power, and due process fields, where the precedents themselves pointed both ways, should create little trouble.

But the balance in favor of the laws in such cases as these was precarious. The affirmative judgments were made possible in both decisions by a bare majority of five including the Chief Justice and a new appointee, Owen Roberts. The four other judges had joined in bitter dissents, rejecting the idea that emergency can affect constitutional results (the Court must not "yield to the voice of an impatient majority when stirred by distressful exigency") and warning of "the far more serious and dangerous inroads upon the limitations of the Constitution which are almost certain to ensue as a consequence naturally following any step beyond the boundaries fixed by that instrument." Such a call to arms was not likely to have much effect on Stone, Brandeis, and Cardozo, the three firm "liberals," for they had no great regard for the laissez-faire order they were being solicited to protect and at all events they doubted that the constitutional boundaries had ever been as clearly fixed as the quoted sentence implies. But Roberts was considerably less settled in his views, and as the New Deal was revealed in all its terrifying dimensions to the conservatives of the nation, he became ready for persuasion. As for the Chief Justice, he was neither clearly liberal nor stubbornly conservative, but he seemed to be much concerned for the Court's own dignity and was likely sometimes to swing with a conservative majority to avoid the criticism that might follow a five-to-four decision.

In 1935, therefore, the majority shifted, and for two busy terms the Court waged what is surely the most ambitious dragonfight in its long and checkered history. The tension between modesty and temerity was temporarily resolved; the autocratic instinct was triumphant. Negative doctrines that had been accumulating for a century were brought to bear on the New Deal program and on kindred heresies; the affirmative doctrines that might have been invoked to produce contrary results were conveniently ignored or distinguished. And throughout the holocaust perorations from the bench and applause from outside the courtroom made it plain that the myths of judicial supremacy had been translated into reality in the minds of the Court majority. The idea of a changeless Constitution, the idea of judicial review as an exact science, the idea that "dominant opinion" is irrelevant, the idea that a nine-man Court can and should save society from itself and the past from the present—these ideas were no longer rhetoric; they had become the wellsprings of action.

With a salvo of decisions during 1935–36, the Court tore great holes in the New Deal program of recovery legislation. The doctrine of "direct-indirect effects" derived from the *Knight* case was used to help dispose of such major laws as the National Industrial Recovery Act and the Bituminous Coal Act. The distinction between production and commerce, stemming from *Knight* and *Dagenhart*, was used against the Agricultural Adjustment Act, which had sought to regulate farm production. The same law ran afoul of the rule of the Child Labor Tax Case that taxes must not operate as penalties to control what is otherwise beyond congressional reach. The due process clause was present in several decisions though sometimes only murkily visible, and the "sovereign prerogative of choice" which the Court had established in interpretation of that clause was of course here seized upon to negate the legislation. The Tenth Amendment, interpreted as a limit on Congress' delegated power rather than as a prohibition against the exercise of powers not delegated, acted as a makeweight wherever it seemed remotely applicable. Even a doctrine which had never been employed negatively before—and has never been since—had its fleeting moments of effectiveness during those years. The NIRA and the Bituminous Coal Act were condemned because, among other things, they had delegated legislative authority to the executive and thus violated the principle of separation of powers.

The final barrage was fired in June of 1936 as the Court reached the close of its two-year joust with the New Deal, and it was directed against a state law. New York had dared to enact a measure providing minimum wages for women. The legislative draftsmen had tried to meet one of the major objections raised by the Court against the law struck down in the *Adkins* case—that the wage-setting board need not consider the value of services rendered. The New York board was authorized to consider this factor, and it was hoped that the law might thus be saved. But the intransigence of the majority seemed to wax rather than wane with the passing months. Justice Butler now announced as a flat rule "that the state is without power by any form of legislation to prohibit, change or nullify contracts between employers and adult women workers as to the amount of wages to be paid." The argument of the Chief Justice, who dissented, that the *Adkins* precedent need not be followed because of "material differences" in the two laws; the argument of Stone, Brandeis, and Cardozo, also dissenting, that precedent since *Adkins* and "what is more important, reason" support state power to control wages, had no weight for five men now thoroughly deluded by the notion that the welfare state could be judicially throttled and the brave old world of their youth restored.

This New York Minimum Wage decision is a fair example of the judicial attitudes that characterized those two years, and it is an example that merits some reflection. By this time—the spring of 1936—the Court's assault on the New Deal had produced a tempest of antijudicial criticism, and as the presidential campaign of that year whetted political feeling, the critics, and of course the defenders as well, became angrier and more extreme (though the President himself said little in the campaign). Much of the criticism simply reflected the bad old American propensity to traduce the law whenever it conflicts with immediate interests, and perhaps the only thing worth saying about this is that, like most deplorable facts, it cannot be safely ignored. Another line of attack, not always distinguishable but with some claim to respectability as a separate point, was to challenge the Court's right and competence to hinder the democratic will, especially in the economic field. However, the Court had made it plain to the nation long ago that it proposed to play some part in defining government-business relationships, and the nation had tacitly acquiesced. It seems a little hard that the judiciary should now be assailed merely for participating in affairs that had been regarded for almost fifty years as judicial business.

But a telling and legitimate criticism of the Court's attitude can nevertheless be made out. The fault was not that the judges meddled in economic affairs at all, but that they meddled with them on a level too high for judicial governance, and imposed constitutional restraints so rigid that no popular government could tolerate them. As Robert Jackson has said, the anti-New Deal decisions had not:

. . . been confined to the limited issues actually involved in the immediate controversies and the way left clear for the Congress to improve and perfect its remedies. . . . [I]n striking at New Deal laws, the Court allowed its language to run riot. . . . In over-throwing the A.A.A. the Court cast doubt upon all federal aid to agriculture; in laying low the N.R.A., the Court struck at all national effort to maintain fair labor standards; and in outlawing the New York Minimum Wage Law . . . the Court deliberately attempted to outlaw any form of state legislation to protect mini-mum wage standards. The Court not merely challenged the policies of the New Deal but erected judicial barriers to the reasonable exercise of legislative powers, both state and national, to meet the urgent needs of a twentieth-century community.

The historic Court (as distinguished from the Court of myth and rhetoric) had very seldom behaved this way, and the ex-ceptions in the record seemed hardly calculated to inspire im-itation. Even in the modern period the dominant tendency had been to moderate the regulatory movement without attempting to destroy it, to nudge and advise democracy rather than to frustrate it. The majority had for the time being forgotten this, had forgotten that the Constitution's strength was its flexibility and that the Court's own strength rested on a tradition of ju-dicious self-restraint.

The price of forgetfulness threatened to be a high one. Frank-lin Roosevelt was re-elected in November, 1936, by a stunning majority, and, after the dust of the campaign had settled a little, he turned his attention to the hostile Supreme Court, just as

The Judiciary and the Welfare State

Jefferson had in 1801 trained his sights on Marshall and his Federalist brethren. Roosevelt, with characteristic indirection, presented Congress with a judiciary plan that purported to cope with the supposed problem of overcrowded federal court dockets. It would have enabled him to appoint a new judge to supplement any judge over seventy who failed to retire (retirement could not of course be made compulsory, for the Constitution protects judicial tenure "during good behavior"). The significant fact was that the plan would permit the President to appoint six new Supreme Court justices, and thus to insure approval of the New Deal program. It was, as it was called, a "court-packing plan," and its passage would set a precedent from which the institution of judicial review might never recover. It is not too much to say that the ambiguous and delicately balanced American tradition of limited government was mortally endangered by this bill. And it was offered by a President who had just received an overwhelming popular vote of confidence and who had not yet been denied in Congress any of his important demands. Even the five or six judges who had provoked this threat must have slept rather uneasily for a few months.

ECHOES OF THE FUTURE: THE EMERGING PROBLEM
OF CIVIL RIGHTS

Like the scenario writer who leaves the heroine hanging from a cliff while he takes up another thread of the narrative, we must now digress for a time in order to touch on a development contemporary with the events so far described in this chapter. It is a characteristic of history, often noted, that the present bears the seeds of the future; and it is therefore hardly surprising that the Court of this era, even at the height of its concern for economic matters, should have devoted a small but increasing portion of its time to a widely different subject which was destined to loom very large in the judicial world yet to come. The subject was "civil rights," that is, the liberties of man as man and not primarily as an economic animal.

During most of its history, the Court had paid comparatively little attention to this problem. The Bill of Rights, it will be remembered, had been held inapplicable to the states in 1833. That meant that free expression (Amendment I) and the personal procedural rights connected with arrest and trial (Amendments IV–VIII) could be abridged by the states without raising a federal constitutional question. The ratification of the Fourteenth Amendment in 1868 had created some doubts on this score, but the *Slaughter-House* decision in 1873 had rejected the contention that the privileges or immunities clause protected such rights.

Ten years later it was held in *Hurtado* v. *California* that the due process clause did not require the states to conform to the Bill of Rights in their criminal procedures, and as late as 1922 the Court denied that the Amendment restricted the states in dealing with freedom of expression. As for the equal protection clause, it had been used a few times to invalidate explicit racial discrimination in state law, but its effectiveness in deterring Jim Crow had been at best marginal. Like the due process clause it had been chiefly important in this era as a shield for business enterprise.

The states, then, were for some time relatively unconfined by constitutional doctrine in the civil rights field. On the other hand the national government had so far had little occasion to encroach on civil rights except in wartime, for police regulation that raised questions of this kind was left almost exclusively to the states. Given these facts, it is easy to see why civil rights cases had been a minor item on the Court's docket.

But now logic was working on behalf of civil rights. And although Justice Holmes was no doubt right when he once remarked that logic is not the "life of the law," still logic must not be thought of as irrelevant to the judicial process. The Court had provided the businessman with a generous measure of protection under the Fourteenth Amendment, and particularly the due process clause. Could it really be successfully contended that the "liberty" mentioned in that clause meant the liberty of economic man, and that only? Was there any rational basis for setting economic freedom so high above such basic rights as the right to a fair trial or liberty of expression? And if not, was it possible to maintain a constitutional discrimination against those rights for very long? In a way the development of the due process clause to protect economic rights made the ultimate protection of other rights logically inescapable.

The force of this logic was strengthened, it should be said, by certain personal factors in the 1920's and 30's, notably the presence on the Court of such brilliant libertarians as Holmes and Brandeis. And the First World War and the Russian Revolution played their part in precipitating the growth of constitutional doctrine, for they led to an assortment of state and federal laws infringing on freedom of expression, and the enforcement of these laws thrust the whole question into the judiciary's hands.

The free speech story properly begins in 1919 when the Court was presented with a constitutional claim brought by a man being punished under the federal Espionage Act of 1917 for mailing antidraft pamphlets to draftees. The defendant argued that his right to distribute such pamphlets was protected against national action by the First Amendment, but Justice Holmes for the Court rejected the claim. This speech is not protected, said Holmes, because it is used in such circumstances and is of such a nature as to create "a clear and present danger" of "substantive evils that Congress has a right to prevent" (that is, obstruction of the draft and mutiny in the armed forces). It followed of course that the Constitution *did* protect speech which did *not* present such a clear and present danger. Thus, although the individual conviction was here upheld, Holmes had scotched an old and persistent idea that the protection of the First Amendment was very narrow, and had committed the Court to an essentially libertarian formula for determining when speech may be abridged (*Schenck* v. *United States*).

The *Schenck* case involved a federal law, and the question of whether the free speech guaranties applied to the states by way of the Fourteenth Amendment was still comparatively untouched. However, the Court in 1925, confronted by a New York law punishing "criminal anarchy," declared "we may and do assume" that freedom of speech and press "are protected by the due process clause of the Fourteenth Amendment from impairment by the States." This was said with an offhandedness reminiscent of the concession in 1886 that corporations are persons in the meaning of the Amendment; and it was to be no less important in the long run. Again, as in *Schenck*, the particular prosecution was upheld, and the majority in fact repudiated the clear and present danger rule, holding that speech could be punished even if the danger of evil results was remote and conjectural. Nonetheless, the principle was now established that state action infringing free expression raised a federal constitutional question, and cases began making their way to the Court in increasing number. In 1931 the Court made its first important ruling against a state law in this field. Evidently a whole new dimension of constitutional jurisprudence had been opened up.

Meanwhile a somewhat similar development had been running its course in connection with the procedural rights of fair trial for accused persons. Although it had been held that the states were not bound by the specific procedural mandates of the Bill of Rights (for instance, they need not provide grand jury indictment as required by Amendment V) the Court had never quite gone so far as to say that the Fourteenth Amendment set no restrictions on state criminal procedures. The formula, stated in 1908, was that a procedural right was protected against state action only if it was "a fundamental principle of liberty and justice which inheres in the very idea of free government." This might seem an empty incantation, particularly since for a long time no decision upholding such a right was handed down. But in the 1920's the Court began to pour some content into it, for much the same reasons that prompted the concomitant drift toward protection of free expression; and in the early 1930's it was clearly held that state denials of the right to counsel and state use of forced confessions had offended this canon of due process. "The rack and the torture chamber," remarked Chief Justice Hughes, "may not be substituted for the witness stand."

As for the problem of racial discrimination in this period, it is hard to find the signs of doctrinal growth that are discernible in the fields of free expression and procedural rights (though it is perhaps worth remarking that the right-to-counsel case and the forced-confession case just mentioned, involved Negroes in the South). The Court had not yet challenged the doctrine that state law could require separation of races in schools, parks, and other facilities, so long as the accommodations provided were substantially equal. Indeed the standard of equality required was still very loose. The states had encountered a judicial setback or two in their attempts to exclude Negroes from the election process and from white residential areas, but by a modest amount of ingenuity they were able to evade these rulings with the acquiescence of the Court. Jim Crow was still constitutional.

But anyone able to think analogically might predict that he would have his judicial troubles before long. The logical process that had helped impel the Court to move from protection of economic liberty to protection of free expression and fair trial was equally relevant to the next step—the judicial defense of the right to racial equality. It would be too much to say that any of these developments became factually inevitable simply because the natural trend of logic supported them. Indeed the constitutional protection provided for these crucial rights was still, in spite of logic, skimpy and occasional. But the path was now open, in case the course of other historical events should provide a stimulus, for the Court to tread it more frequently.

THE CONSTITUTIONAL REVOLUTION OF 1937

In fact the occasion was already in the making, and, as it turned out, the time was nearly ripe. Having constructed with the greatest of pains a doctrinal tradition that allowed judicial intervention in economic affairs, and having administered those doctrines with reasonable discretion for some years, the Court had finally and dangerously overstepped the line that marks the limits of its authority. At a moment when the political pressure for economic legislation was greater than ever before, the Court had chosen to call a halt; at a moment when the Constitution's famous flexibility was most required, the Court had chosen to regard judicial review as the automatic application of static principles. The depression, and the New Deal which was its reflex, were forces too cosmic for those Canutes to withstand. Finally, the waves dislodged even the partial and contingent grip on economic affairs that the judiciary had once enjoyed. If the judges had stood firm in the position they assumed in 1935–36, there seems a good chance they would have been submerged altogether.

But they did not stand firm, or at any rate Justice Roberts did not, and he was the man who most mattered. The Roosevelt electoral victory in the fall of 1936 was impressive enough to convince all but those who would not listen that the American people wanted the New Deal. An outbreak of labor-management disputes, some of them accompanied by violence, had graphically illustrated the grim fact that the national economic dilemma was still very acute. On February 5, 1937, the President's "court-packing plan" had been set before Congress. No one, perhaps not even Justice Roberts, could say which of these circumstances was decisive for him; but it is hard to doubt that they played a part in the new tone of judicial decision that began to be sounded in the early months of that year.

It was first heard on March 29, 1937, less than two months after the Court plan was submitted and while the war of words over it was raging. The Court was presented with a state minimum wage law applying to women and minors, a law not materially different from the one overturned in the New York Minimum Wage Case only nine months before. But now, by a vote of five to four, the judges upheld the law, rejecting both the

Adkins precedent of 1923 and the New York decision. Chief Justice Hughes for the majority denied that freedom of contract was especially sanctified in the American system of constitutional restraints, declared that the Court must take judicial notice of the depression prostrating the nation, and found without difficulty that a minimum wage law was reasonably related to the legitimate end of preserving the workers' health. Justice Roberts, who had seen the matter differently nine months earlier, silently concurred.

Observers were still recovering from their surprise two weeks later when the Court astonished them again. This time the law in question was one of those major statutes that Congress had passed to cope with the national economic impasse—the National Labor Relations Act. In four decisions the law was upheld in spite of the fact that it controlled labor relations in production industries and in spite of the reiteration only a year before of the doctrine that production affected commerce "indirectly" and was therefore immune from congressional regulation. The direct-indirect distinction was in effect discarded. Again the vote was five to four; again the switch in the position of Justice Roberts tipped the scales.

Finally, on May 24, the Court backtracked dramatically once more. The Social Security Act of 1935 was for most exponents of laissez faire the very symbol of the paternalist theory of government which the New Deal represented and which they found so odious. Moreover, it offended the old negativisms of constitutional jurisprudence in a multiple sense, for it used the tax power to accomplish social ends and induced the states to participate in the plan and conform to nationally prescribed standards. On the authority of the *Butler* decision of 1936, this apparent encroachment on the states' reserved powers was most dubious, but again the Court upheld the law, again by a vote of five to four. Justice Roberts, the author of the *Butler* decision, had again changed his mind.

Meanwhile the controversy over the court-packing plan had been bitterly fought in the Congress and in the forum of public opinion. But although the drive to enact the President's proposal continued after the decisions just described, it had lost much of its force and more of its point. In the long run it failed, and the failure is a significant testimonial to the prestige that attached to the Court's Constitution in the American mind. Not all the influence of a master politician in the prime of his popularity was quite enough to carry a program that would impair judicial review. Yet the Court's defenders were hardly entitled to be complacent. The Court's recantation had helped save the day; certain fortuitous circumstances relating to legislative strategy had made a difference, too. The danger had been great. Even a close call can teach a lesson.

Constitutional doctrine emerged from those months of crisis profoundly altered. The Court's relationship to the American polity had undergone a fundamental change. Quite probably the judges themselves did not understand how great a withdrawal was portended by their about-face in 1937. But within a few years it would be plain to all that another constitutional era had ended and a new one had begun. As the Civil War had settled the basic question underlying the nation-state conflict, so the Depression and the New Deal had resolved the basic question of economic control. Significant economic issues remained to be decided, of course, even after the nation had made the basic decision against laissez faire, but the Court by its own intransigence had disqualified itself to assist in the process by which those decisions were reached. When the extreme negativist position of 1935–36 was forsaken, as it had to be, the Court could find no stopping place short of abdication.

One aspect of the 1937 judicial revolution then was full-scale rejection of the idea that economic legislation was open to constitutional challenge on the basis of its "unreasonableness." The businessman, so long the Court's darling, was shorn of his constitutional fleece and now faced popular sovereignty protected by nothing save his own ample private resources. The second aspect was judicial acceptance of the idea, almost always implicit in the Court's actual past behavior, that constitutional rules must be flexible within broad limits and that as Justice Stone had put it, "the only check upon our own exercise of power is our own sense of self-restraint." The judicial sovereignty of rhetoric and myth, inexorably holding an irresponsible nation to an objectively ascertainable path of constitutional duty, had died the death with *Lochner*, *Adkins*, and *United States* v. *Butler*.

The Court therefore faced a future in which its interests of seventy years past were no longer relevant and in which myths of even longer standing would be deeply impaired. But recent experience, with all its hazards, had not stifled the remarkable institutional vitality that had sustained the Court throughout its stormy history. The old interests and values were gone, but a new set would arise to replace them. It is significant and far from a coincidence that 1937, the year of the great recantation, was also the year in which the Court revived, by implication at least, the clear and present danger test as a standard for judging questions of free speech (*Herndon* v. *Lowry*). The same year saw the doctrine of judicial control over state criminal procedures stated more explicitly than ever before (*Palko* v. *Connecticut*). One year later the Court for the first time enforced the equal protection clause on behalf of Negro rights in the field of education (*Missouri* v. *Canada*). With or without myths, the future was on its way.

VII

The Modern Court and
Modern America

The situation of the Supreme Court immediately after the constitutional revolution of 1937 was in many ways analogous to its situation at the close of the Civil War. Then as now prodigious national events had conspired to decide the question which had heretofore been the main focus of the Court's interest; then as now the nation's decision had left the judges in the status of men who are threatened by technological unemployment. In 1866 as in 1938 the Court was still smarting from wounds incurred by its own rashness. An observer viewing the Court at either of these hours in its history might have felt warranted to predict that judicial review had reached its twilight period, that the Court's career as an important factor in the American political process was drawing to a close.

But such an observer making such a judgment would be reckoning without the durability and elasticity of the institution Marshall and Taney and Field and Holmes had nurtured. He would be leaving out of account the qualities of the American political character that had led to the development of judicial review in the first place and had sustained and encouraged its continuance for so many years. In 1937 the people had again given testimony to the existence of that quality by refusing to abet an assault on the Court even though it was carried on in their name to chastise the Court for thwarting their will. With such a fund of support to draw on and with their august tradition to inspirit them, the judges were not apt to recede into humble obscurity unless they had no other choice.

If they were to play a real part, however, in the modern affairs of the Republic, they needed to evolve a new sphere of interests and a new set of values to guide them within that sphere. The problems of their past—the nation-state problem, the business-government problem—had successively been snatched from their grasp by history. It was necessary once more to reorient the Court's interests, to formulate another system of judicial values, and to develop a role for the Court in these new terms.

The interest that was to dominate this third great era of judicial history was, as has been intimated in the preceding chapter, civil rights. The Court which had once been primarily occupied with the nation-state relationship and, some time later, with the business-government relationship now became more and more concerned with the relationship between the individual and government. And the values that it now chose to cherish and defend were those embraced by Justice Frankfurter's phrase: "the free play of the human spirit."

History, which had displaced the Court's old ideal of free enterprise, was quick to provide material to fill the gap. The rise of totalitarianism created new problems for America and cast a different light on problems that were old. The nation faced mortal threats of a degree it had not known since the Civil War and of a kind that it had never known before. The freedom of political dissent had formerly been preserved without much difficulty simply because there had been little occasion for government to challenge it; but now fear generated repressive political impulses.

Yet at the same time the spectacle of the police state in Germany and Russia and elsewhere caused many Americans to revere freedom of expression more consciously than they had in the past and to resist attempts to inhibit it. The racist doctrines of Adolf Hitler and the frightful implementation of those doctrines in Nazi policy helped provoke a feeling of dissatisfaction and guilt over America's own patterns of race discrimination. The right of fair trial, once taken for granted, assumed new layers of significance in the minds of men repelled by the totalitarian image. For some, the concern for the civil rights issue was enhanced by awareness that America had become willy-nilly the leader of the free world and must set a responsible leader's example. And because these three categories of rights were logically hard to separate, alertness to one tended to stimulate alertness to all, so that they mutually animated one another. This is how self-consciousness about the civil rights problem was heightened in the 1930's and 40's and how the Supreme Court was impelled to focus on that problem. For, as history has repeatedly attested, the members of the Supreme Court are children of their times, and a chronicle of Court doctrine tends to be, in a general way, an intellectual history of America.

However, in the post-1937 period as in earlier periods, the

The Modern Court and Modern America

Court's adoption of a new congeries of interests and values created the problem of working out a judicial role that would best serve these new purposes. The doctrines of the past, forged to serve past aims, had to be reconstructed, as the due process clause for example was altered in the 1880's and 90's to suit the circumstances of that era. The judges had to rethink the question of the Court's place in the American polity, to feel their way to a *modus operandi* that would enable the Court to defend its new values with reasonable effectiveness but would simultaneously take due account of the limits of judicial control.

And the problem of role definition was all the more acute, as was suggested at the close of the last chapter, because the Court's own behavior and a generation of criticism by "judicial realists" had undermined the myths of judicial supremacy and objectivity. The Court of the early twentieth century had flagrantly confirmed the thesis of this school of critics by refusing to bind itself to objective standards in any of the great areas of judicial supervision. The judges who came to the supreme bench after the constitutional revolution (Justice Van Devanter was the first of the old guard to resign, to be succeeded by Justice Black) were men who had been reared in that school, and they joined Justice Stone, one of its leading spokesmen. They had reason to be more explicitly aware than perhaps any Court of the past had been that theirs was "not the only agency of government that must be assumed to have capacity to govern" and that "the criterion of constitutionality is not whether [judges] believe the law to be for the public good." Their task of finding a place for themselves in the new order was made more difficult, though perhaps clearer, by this fact that self-deception was no longer so reliable an ally.

The first order of business was to convince the informed public, including an almost incorrigibly hopeful legal fraternity, that the Court really meant what it implied in 1937: that economic issues were no longer of much constitutional relevance. Businessmen were so accustomed to the Court's favors that they found it hard to adjust to the new dispensation. Yet the judicial drift quickly became unmistakable, as the old negative doctrines were discarded or refined to the point of disappearance. The restrictive interpretations of the tax power, which had served so well in the Child Labor Tax Case and the AAA case, had been pretty well scuttled in the spring of 1937 by the Social Security Act decisions. Congress could tax and spend for the "general welfare" (Art. I, sec. 8 [1]) and the fact that a tax controlled local affairs would make no constitutional difference so long as the general welfare, as Congress saw it, would be served. Even the ancient ban on "intergovernmental taxation" was drastically moderated in 1939. The Court formally repudiated Marshall's aphorism that "the power to tax involves the power to destroy," and thus wiped out more than a century's accumulation of intricate doctrine. State and nation could now tax each other's instrumentalities so long as the tax was neither discriminatory nor "unduly" burdensome.

In the commerce clause field, too, the hardy old negativisms were mowed down with rude abandon. The second Agricultural Adjustment Act of 1938 was upheld despite the fact that it excluded "harmless" commodities from interstate commerce by establishing quotas on the amount that could be sold, and indirectly regulated production. In 1942 the Court sustained an even more venturesome amendment which imposed limits on wheat grown for on-the-farm uses even though no part of it was sold in interstate trade. A year before it had upheld the Fair Labor Standards Act which prescribed wages and hours for firms engaged in or producing goods for interstate commerce. The idea that production was beyond congressional reach, the distinction between direct and indirect effects were all given the quietus. As Justice Jackson remarked for a unanimous bench in the wheat quotas case: "The Court's recognition of the relevance of the economic effects in the application of the Commerce Clause . . . has made the mechanical application of legal formulas no longer feasible" (*Wickard* v. *Filburn*).

It was now evident that Congress could reach just about any commercial subject it might want to reach and could do to that subject just about anything it was likely to want to do, whether for economic, humanitarian, or other purposes. The decisions, it is true, offer a hint that some regulations might go too far, that some local activities might be exempt from federal control because their effect on interstate commerce was not substantial. But these hints were small comfort to businessmen appealing for present relief; and business was thoroughly warranted in inferring that the constitutional distinction between intrastate and interstate commerce was no longer a practical limit on federal power.

This was a bitter pill to swallow for those who had benefited from the Old Court's solicitous jurisprudence, but the enfeeblement of the due process clause as a substantive limit on economic legislation was even more dismaying. The post-1937 Court in effect adopted the criterion urged by Justice Holmes in his classic series of dissents during the first three decades of the century. It was authoritatively expressed in 1938 by Justice Stone in *United States* v. *Carolene Products:*

> . . . regulatory legislation affecting ordinary commercial trans-actions is not to be pronounced unconstitutional unless in the light of the facts made known or generally assumed it is of such a character as to preclude the assumption that it rests upon some rational basis within the knowledge and experience of the legislators.

It is hard to conceive a law so patently unreasonable that it would fail under this test, and it is therefore not surprising that the Court since 1937 has never encountered one. And the Court showed itself ready to make a loose standard even looser by stretching its imagination to the limits to find *some* sensible reason for the law and impute that motive to the legislative authors. Not even the most optimistic litigant could persuade himself for very long after 1938 that an economic statute would be held unreasonable on substantive grounds.

Of course the Court had always paid lip service to the principle that a law should be presumed valid "until its viola-tion of the Constitution is proved beyond reasonable doubt" (*Ogden* v. *Saunders*, 1827). But the judges had breached this precept in such decisions as *Lochner*, *Adkins*, and the anti–New Deal cases, for the very good reason that compliance with it would have forced them to uphold the questioned laws. Now this "presumption of constitutionality" was reinstated with a vengeance, and the extreme form it took is a measure of the Court's determination to have done with economic affairs in the due process area. A state law forbidding women to work as barmaids; another forcing employers to pay employees for hours not worked on election day; still another in effect restricting the river-boat pilot profession to relatives and friends of present pilots—all these were upheld against due process and equal protection attack. The ghosts of Field and Peckham and Sutherland must have stirred restlessly to see freedom of contract so hardly used. But it was not their shades, but those of Holmes and Brandeis that now dominated the course of decision. Constitutional laissez faire was as dead as mutton.

This is not to say that the post-1937 Court was able to ignore the economic world altogether. Though substantive due process in this area was virtually abandoned, the older and historically more legitimate concept of procedural due process survived, and a businessman could still hope for constitutional recourse if, for example, a law took his property without notice or fair hearing. And although the commerce power of Congress was no longer subject to serious constitutional question, the problem of whether state action impinged on interstate commerce (the old problem of the *Cooley* case) still absorbed a respectable share of the Court's attention. The principle seemed to be that such a state law was acceptable if it did not discriminate against interstate commerce (that is, if it treated the state's own commerce and that of the nation equally) and if the Court felt that the state interest served by the law outweighed "whatever national interest there might be in the prevention of state restrictions." But this form of supervision over economic matters, though not insignificant, is a far cry from the sovereignty once claimed over the whole business-government relationship. And the crucial point is that the Court's doctrines were no longer set up as a barrier against regulations as such. The question of whether America should become a welfare state was now referred strictly to the political branches of government.

HUMILITY VERSUS PRIDE: INTERNATIONAL AGREEMENTS AND EXECUTIVE POWER

All this suggests a judiciary overwhelmed by considerations of modesty and resolved to interfere as little as possible in the conduct of government, particularly when national power is involved. And the impression seems confirmed by certain other doctrinal tendencies of the era. The rule against undue delegation of legislative power, invoked by the Old Court to help extinguish the New Deal, was now so attenuated that it took on the quality of a moral admonition rather than a legal limitation. In a case involving the validity of federal price control legislation, for example, the Court upheld the law even though it empowered the administrator to issue price regulations subject only to the requirement that they tend to effectuate the very broad purposes of the Act (essentially to prevent inflation), that they be "fair and equitable" (whatever that may mean), and that the administrator "so far as practicable" give "due consideration" to the prices prevailing in October, 1941. The arguments of the judges in the NRA case almost ten years before, that executive discretion under the recovery act was "virtually unfettered" and not "canalized within banks that keep it from overflowing," seem equally apposite here. But now only Justice Roberts dissented from the holding that the standards provided for the administrator's guidance were constitutionally adequate. Even before the 1937 revolution the Court had approved the delegation of very broad discretion to the President in the field of foreign affairs (*United States* v. *Curtiss-Wright*, 1936). Now it appeared that the rule was similarly permissive when applied to domestic administration.

Nor was the conduct of foreign policy hampered by other sorts of judicially contrived restraints. As long ago as 1920, Justice Holmes, speaking for the Court, had declared that a treaty might accomplish results that a mere act of Congress could not, that the limits of the Constitution applied "in a different way" when the treaty-making power was called into question (Art. II, sec. 2 [2]). In view of this decision and in view of the fact that no treaty had ever been held to exceed constitutional bounds, some alarmed observers have suspected that no such bounds exist as far as the judiciary is concerned. And their apprehension about the danger of arbitrary government in the foreign affairs area was hardly quelled by a 1942 decision holding that an "executive agreement" made by the President with a foreign government (without the concurrence of the Senate, which is required for a treaty) was paramount to state laws.

It is a pretty safe bet that the Court would invalidate a treaty or executive agreement that bartered away all or part of the Bill of Rights; the power to make such international compacts could not avail to deprive Americans of free speech or fair trial. But aside from such an unlikely eventuality, it must be conceded that the chances of judicial interference with this authority are very remote. In connection with the power over foreign affairs, as in connection with national power over economic affairs, the modern Court has for practical purposes abandoned the concept of judicial control and has thrust the responsibility for worrying about constitutional limits on the shoulders of the President and Congress. The argument for this policy of abnegation is that government must have great leeway to act effectively in these two intricate and technical fields, and that judicial review is too restricted in its sources of information and too cumbersome in its procedures to supervise such action adequately. The danger is of course that the other branches of government will fail to assume the constitutional responsibility which the Court has tendered to them, and will interpret the assignment as a license to act arbitrarily. But for better or for worse the fact remains that these two great and increasingly important areas of public affairs are now subject to constitutional limits only in the sense that the British Parliament is constitutionally limited, that is, by legislative and executive self-restraint and by the force of public opinion.

Yet in spite of all these evidences of judicial humility in these areas, it would be an error to assume that the judiciary had lost self-confidence altogether as a result of its chastening experience in the 1930's. One of the best single illustrations of the fact that it had not is to be found in the Steel Seizure decision of 1952. In order to avert a nationwide steel strike which he thought would imperil America's defense, President Truman had seized the steel mills on behalf of the United States government by executive order. Mr. Truman's authority to take such action was not specifically granted by statute, and his right, if any, to seize the mills, therefore, had to rest on the old idea that the President possesses certain "inherent powers" to act for the national welfare even without specific statutory authorization. The Court had tacitly recognized some such prerogative in a few opinions during its history, but in general the concept of inherent power had developed extra-judicially as a result of presidential practice and congressional acquiescence. The Court of the past had seemed to feel about this question the way the modern Court felt about the commerce power and the treaty power—that it was best left to the political branches of government.

The Modern Court and Modern America

But now the Court of 1952, otherwise so skittish about intruding in economic affairs, undertook to mediate this hot dispute between the President and one of the great economic forces of the nation. The "opinion of the Court" by Justice Black boldly held that the President had no authority to act as he did because the subject was within the sphere of Congress' authority; when the President entered that sphere without congressional permission, he violated the principle of separation of powers. Some of the other majority judges did not concur in this definition of executive power that would confine it to matters outside Congress' range (what those matters might be would be hard to say considering the modern scope of legislative power). But they did argue that the President had erred in this instance because, said they, certain federal statutes forbid Mr. Truman to do what he did, and surely inherent executive power, even if there is such a thing, does not license the President to violate statutes.

To that proposition all the judges agreed, and so would most observers, including President Truman (who contended that the supposedly prohibitory statutes were being wrongly interpreted). But such a consensus should not obscure the very real question of whether the Supreme Court should have tried to resolve a controversy so heatedly fought at the bar of public opinion, so loaded with immediate and grave national consequences. At all events the decision reminds us that judicial self-restraint is not the only theme of the modern era. The modern judges have been torn, as were their predecessors of the early twentieth century, between the impulse to wield the scepter and the impulse to remain "lions under the throne." A similar tension has been set up; similar lines of division have been drawn. And the Steel Seizure case represents, as *Adkins* did, a

breaking-out and temporary assertion of the old urge to monarchize.

THE COURT SEEKS A ROLE: THE PROBLEM OF
FREEDOM OF EXPRESSION

The tension between the instinct to dominate and the instinct
to forbear has been most clearly evident in connection with the
subject the modern Court seems to care most about—civil rights.
And the competing considerations that have helped to generate
the tensions here have been by no means easy to resolve. On
the one hand, there has been the feeling, more or less deeply
shared by all the modern judges, that "those liberties of the
individual which history has attested as the indispensable conditions of an open as against a closed society come to the Court
with a momentum for respect lacking when appeal is made to
liberties which derive merely from shifting economic arrange-
ments." The words are those of Justice Frankfurter and some
of the reasons for the rise of the sentiment have already been
discussed. It can be judicially implemented, as Justice Stone
once intimated, by subjecting to "more exacting judicial scrutiny" legislation "which restricts the political processes which
can ordinarily be expected to bring about repeal of undesirable
legislation" and which reflect "prejudices against discrete and
insular minorities" (*United States* v. *Carolene Products Co.*,
1938). Coupled with and supporting this modern concern for
civil rights as a value, has been the tradition, running back to
Marshall and beyond, that the Court has the power and duty
to right wrongs, to translate its moral convictions into constitutional limitations.

On the other hand, of course, there were ranged all the notions about judicial humility that had been generated by the iconoclastic movement of the preceding decades, and an awareness—on the part of at least some of the judges—that the historic Court had usually accomplished more by moderation than by arrogance. These notions, well-grounded enough in any event, could be reinforced in the post-1937 era by a special circumstance of the times: the fact that *crisis* seemed to have become a chronic condition. The concept of constitutional limitation had never functioned very well in emergencies. In moments of great peril, when the temper of the populace was likely to be superheated, the judicial tendency had been to withdraw and wait for more auspicious, normal times. This had been Marshall's policy in the dangerous years after the Jeffersonian revolution, and it had been adopted by the Court with varying degrees of frankness in critical periods that followed. The exceptions have not made very pleasant readings for the Court's friends. Judicial attempts to control policy in such times have seldom been ultimately very successful. In the years after 1937, as wars hot and cold posed awesome problems and frayed public nerves, the case for judicial modesty was not easy to refute. But neither was it easy to dismiss the argument that civil rights are the essence of democratic government and that the Court must do its best to preserve them. The difficulty was to decide what its best was.

The Court's erratic pattern of response to the issue of free expression illustrates these judicial perplexities with special force. In the first few years after 1937, the judges seemed inclined to stand the old constitutional order on its head, and to assert a power of review over free speech statutes that was unmodified by considerations of judicial self-restraint. Holmes's clear and present danger principle, ignored by the majority since 1919, was now revitalized and put forward as a talismanic standard to be applied to all categories of free speech problems. Moreover the Holmesian rubric was strengthened in its negative implications by an amendment that had been proposed by Justice Brandeis in a 1927 concurring opinion. In order to sustain a statute inhibiting freedom of speech, he had suggested, the Court must find a clear and present danger of a *serious* evil; "prohibition of free speech and assembly is a measure so stringent that it would not be appropriate as the means for averting a relatively trivial harm to society" (*Whitney* v. *California*).

Now the rhetoric of clear and present danger in this form expresses well enough some of the factors that might guide the citizen or his legislative representative in deciding whether free expression should be restrained; and it is no doubt advisable that the judicial process take account of these factors, too. But in some of the early decisions of this era the Court gave the impression that its opinion about clear and present danger was the only one that counted and that the "presumption of constitutionality," once denied in *Lochner* and *Adkins* to statutes touching freedom of contract, was now denied to those infringing freedom of speech. The doctrine seemed to be, pressing Justice Stone's *Carolene Products* logic hard, that free expression (including of course religious expression) occupied a "preferred position" in America's constellation of constitutional rights, and that government action impinging on it was presumptively invalid. Armed with these concepts and attitudes, the Court disapproved a considerable number of state actions, including a law forbidding peaceful picketing, another requiring union organizers to register, state court contempt holdings against those who were accused of using the press to influence judicial proceedings, and a state law requiring school children to salute the flag in spite of their contrary religious convictions.

Most of the state measures invalidated in this period were foolish or pernicious, and some of them might well have been overthrown even by a judiciary fully alive to the virtue of modesty. But the decisions nevertheless were vulnerable to criticism on at least two grounds. In the first place the opinions that accompanied them were barren of evidence that the Court was taking adequate account of the legislature's claim to share in "the power to govern." It is one thing to decide that a state action exceeds the bounds of reason and quite another, as Sir Frederick Pollock once said, to treat the legislature "like an inferior court which had to give proof of its competence." The judges had long ago been powerfully admonished by Justice Holmes: "It must be remembered that legislators are the ultimate guardians of the liberties and welfare of the people in quite as great a degree as the courts." Now, with respect to free speech statutes, that reminder seemed to be forgotten.

But second, and in practical terms even more important, the opinions assumed a role for the Court and a rigidity of constitutional limits that could not be sustained in the face of real adversity. The idea seemed to be that the Court would hold government action aimed at free speech to the same kind of strict substantive limits that had been applied, in *Adkins* and similar cases, to inhibitions on freedom of contract. This failed to reckon with the possibility of extreme public need or (what is pretty much the same thing as far as the Court is concerned) extreme public demand for repressive legislation. The doctrines and assumptions of these cases proved no more tenable as the totalitarian threat became acute than the similar doctrines and assumptions of *Adkins* had been tenable in the Great Depression.

What was especially unfortunate about all this is that it left the Court unprepared to cope with adversity when it did come. Instead of working out a viable judicial attitude toward infringements on free speech, the Court had enunciated a policy of flat negation; and when that policy had to be abandoned, there was nothing to take its place except uncriticial acquiescence to the legislative will. Growing national awareness of the totalitarian threat in the years after 1945 generated a national mood toward "subversion" that sometimes approached hysteria. Government action in response to that mood was often savagely hostile to freedom of expression. If the judges had been thinking their problem through in the years just preceding, they might have been ready with an approach that could have moderated the tempest and contributed usefully to the resolution of a grave national quandary. But since most of them had been orating rather than thinking, and since the uncompromising policy set forth in the oratory had become impossible, the only alternative seemed to be judicial collapse. At no time in its history had the Court been able to maintain a position squarely opposed to a strong popular majority. There was no reason to expect that it could do so now. In contrast to the negativism of the first few post-1937 years, the Court now became so tolerant of governmental restriction on freedom of expression as to suggest that it was abdicating the field.

The two decisions that exemplified this phase of modern judicial history were *American Communications Ass'n* v. *Douds* (1950) and *Dennis* v. *United States* (1951). Both involved national statutes visiting penalties on Communists, and in both the Court upheld the government actions, painfully swallowing its brave libertarian protestations of a few years before. However the most troubling thing about the decisions was not so much that they sustained the government, but that they came close to abandoning altogether the concept of judicial limitation. The *Douds* opinion by Chief Justice Vinson suggested, about as strongly as words might, that Congress could use the commerce power to interfere with free speech and association without fear of *any* constitutional hindrance. In *Dennis* the language was somewhat more guarded, but the result was not very different. The clear and present danger doctrine, put forward in recent opinions as a kind of universal rule, was now redefined in such a way as to make it meaningless and, for practical purposes, useless. The Court's role as the uncompromising defender of liberty against all comers, also so recently asserted and reasserted, was likewise abandoned. The implication was that judicial review could contribute nothing to the solution of America's "subversion problem" and that the Court's only course was to stand aside while the winds howled on Capitol Hill and elsewhere.

However, it turned out that another phase in this history of judicial responses was already taking shape at the very time that these spectacularly acquiescent decisions were handed down. For one thing, though shying off from the issue of subversion, the Court had continued to widen the area of freedom in cases involving what might be called "non-seditious free speech." For the first time in history, for example, the Court had overturned state laws censoring magazines and motion pictures. These decisions were couched in careful language; they did not condemn all censorship per se. But they made it clear that censorship does raise a constitutional question and thereby opened up a whole new area of judicial supervision. A comparable development was meanwhile taking place in cases involving both the "free exercise of religion" and the "no establishment" clauses of the First Amendment. The substance of those clauses had been held to be binding on the states by way of the Fourteenth Amendment. Now the Court struck down state aid to religion on the ground that it breached the "wall of separation" between church and state and on the ground that it infringed religious liberty. Again the decisions were so framed as to leave some leeway for state policy; but again it had been made plain that a subject highly relevant to free expression was subject to constitutional control.

In the second place, as public enthusiasm for domestic red-hunting subsided somewhat, and as the Court had a chance to take new bearings, the outlines of a mature policy in the subversive field began to emerge. In the stormy times of the *Douds* and *Dennis* cases, the judges seemed to have forgotten that there is more than one way to skin a cat. Awed by the dimensions of the subversion problem and loath to challenge the substantive power of Congress on an issue related to national defense, they had chosen to do nothing. As their history should have informed them, however, there is a middle way between over-assertiveness and abdication even when congressional statutes are concerned. National laws must be *interpreted* by the federal courts, and judicial misgivings about the wisdom or necessity of such laws can be expressed through "the alchemy of construction." In short, the Supreme Court can often so interpret a law invading free speech as to moderate its virulence. This serves to remind Congress and country that a zone of doubt has been entered and encourages them to take a second look at their problem. Yet it leaves Congress free to correct the judicial gloss if convinced, after reflection, that a harsher interpretation should prevail. A further advantage from the viewpoint of democratic values is that the approach focuses responsibility by requiring Congress to speak unmistakably when it wishes to impinge on freedom of expression.

In the 1950's the Supreme Court rediscovered this item in its bag of tricks and began to use it to exert a significant influence on national policy relating to subversion and allied phenomena. Perhaps the most far-reaching case in point was *Pennsylvania* v. *Nelson* which involved the jailing of a Communist party member under a state sedition law. By this time (1956) the national government had added three major peacetime sedition statutes to its books, and most of the states had been stirred by the postwar excitement over such matters to elaborate and intensify their own antisubversive programs. This added up to a bewildering number and variety of governmental restrictions on freedom of expression, and in the *Nelson* case the Court simplified the situation by wiping the state laws, temporarily at least, off the slate. The Court argued that Congress, in passing the national sedition laws, had superseded the state laws by implication. Since the problem dealt with by the laws—national defense—is obviously national in character, there could be no doubt that Congress *could* override state laws if it chose to do so. By holding that the Congress *had* so chosen, the Court threw its weight on the side of rationality and liberty, yet avoided the heavy responsibility of an irrevocable constitutional pronouncement against such state activity.

With respect to free expression, then, the modern Court seems to have established, temporarily at least, a balance between the extremes of judicial supremacy and judicial abdication. Doctrines have been reshaped and jurisdiction widened so as to bring a new range of subjects under potential constitutional control. This development of a jurisprudence of free expression has been in many ways comparable to the development of a jurisprudence of laissez faire in the closing decades of the nineteenth century. And now, as then, the Court, having evolved the tools of judicial supervision, has been faced by the problem of how to use them. The current answer seems to be twofold: government is held to a fairly strict but not inflexible standard in fields unrelated to subversion; in fields that do involve the subversion issue, Congress is left free within wide limits, and the Court employs the device of statutory interpretations to mitigate the asperities of repressive laws and insure that the legislative will is clearly expressed. This adds up to a comparatively modest version of the doctrine of judicial supremacy. It constitutes the judiciary as a significant but not dominant partner in the American governmental enterprise. Throughout the modern period there have been members of the bench who chafed under the limitations of this role and yearned to play a greater part in shaping the decisions of the nation. It remains to be seen whether they will ultimately succeed in launching the Court on one of those campaigns of derring-do that have from time to time marked its history.

JUDICIAL SUCCESSES AND FAILURES: THE PROBLEM OF PROCEDURAL RIGHTS

The modern drive to harry subversives by inhibiting their freedom of expression has also been hampered to some extent by the Supreme Court's insistence that the procedural guarantees of the Constitution must be observed. Like the approach to statutory interpretation just described, this procedural fastidiousness represents a nice compromise between too much judicial review and too little. When Congress is told that it must respect the procedural rights of persons even though they are suspected of subversion, this preserves the substantive power of Congress to accomplish its basic objects and at the same time acts as a reminder that the idea of constitutional limit still lives.

The Court's zeal in enforcing procedural standards has been tempered by an awareness that government needs elbow room to operate effectively, and it is arguable that this spirit of judicial tolerance has sometimes been overdone. During the Second World War, for example, the military authorities (backed, it should be said, by the President and Congress) decided that some 112,000 Japanese-Americans must be moved out of the West Coast military area as a security measure. The decision was carried out in spite of the fact that about 70,000 of the victims were United States citizens and that no crime could be charged, much less proved, against them. The Supreme Court upheld this wholesale invasion of procedural rights, arguing that it could not second-guess the military on a question relating to national defense and calling for swift action. The case provides another illustration—if one is needed—of the proposition that judicial review is likely to be weakest during grave national emergencies. It also illustrates the curious tendency to polarized thinking that occasionally besets the American judiciary. The idea that the Court must either uphold a governmental policy in all respects or disapprove it altogether was controlling in the *Milligan* case in 1866 and in this case almost a century later. Yet the Court's whole history is a refutation of that black-and-white idea.

Procedural rules were sometimes interpreted rather generously in other areas as well. The right against "unreasonable searches and seizures" (Amendment IV) did not avail, for example, to prevent federal officers from searching the premises of an arrested person even though they bore no warrant to conduct the search and there had been ample time to get one before making the arrest. Evidence obtained by wiretapping was not admissible in federal tribunals because wiretapping was forbidden by federal statute, but the Court steadily refused to hold that wiretapping violated the Fourth Amendment, and it allowed the admission of evidence obtained by various hidden listening devices like radio transmitters.

The procedural protection of those threatened by such grave penalties as deportation was not all that it might be. The Court permitted the government to hold a man in prison without bail while deportation proceedings were pending, even though no deportable offense had yet been proved against him and the proceedings might well drag on for years. A federal law of 1954 required witnesses to answer questions that might ordinarily incriminate them and granted them immunity from prosecution on the matters disclosed. The Court upheld the law against the argument that it impaired the privilege against self-incrimination guaranteed by the Fifth Amendment. The statutory immunity from criminal prosecution could not of course protect a man from the other penalties of his testimony, such as loss of employment and "infamy" but the Court declined to extend the right so as to cover such hazards.

Yet the procedural rights that the Court did secure or enlarge during the modern period were by no means insignificant, particularly in their bearing on freedom of expression. In spite of the Immunity Act decision and others which construed the Fifth Amendment narrowly, the Court approached the right against self-incrimination, as Justice Frankfurter said "in a spirit of strict, not lax, observance of the constitutional protection of the individual." The Court made it clear for example in 1950 that the right was available to those who were asked about Communist activities by courts, congressional committees, or any other federal agency. The refusal to enlarge the privilege into a general right of silence or to extend it otherwise by interpretation reflects unwillingness to go forward, not a disposition to go back. And in the field of deportation and denaturalization, although the Court did sometimes uphold rather arbitrary government behavior, it also established in the modern period the important principle that a man threatened by deportation or denaturalization was entitled to *some* procedural rights under the due process clause. The old doctrine, arguably supported by some court decisions, had been that constitutional limits did not apply at all in these areas of governmental power.

Furthermore due process in the procedural sense was increasingly held to be relevant to statutes directly inhibiting freedom of expression. The vice of "vagueness" in a legal prohibition can always be challenged on due process grounds, for a man cannot be fairly punished unless he has a reasonable basis for knowing that his act was forbidden. But vagueness was regarded as particularly objectionable in free speech statutes, and this judicial stand helped to overthrow or discourage the kind of shotgun enactments that legislators sometimes pass, because it takes time and knowledge to draw a statute carefully.

In a similar vein, a "loyalty oath" requirement applied to public college teachers was held invalid on the essentially procedural ground that it penalized innocent as well as knowing membership in "subversive organization" and thus violated due process.

The opinions emphasized that such thoughtlessly broad statutes affected not only the immediate litigants but the atmosphere of freedom generally, because they may "chill that free play of the spirit which all teachers ought especially to cultivate and practice." This decision (*Wiemann* v. *Updegraff*, 1952) was important, too, because it flatly rejected the old, bad idea that "there is no constitutionally protected right to public employment." The government may not exclude a public servant from employment on arbitrary or discriminatory grounds.

This attitude toward procedures, combined with the policy of interpreting free speech laws strictly, enabled the modern Court to reconcile its feelings of modesty with its modern solicitude for individual rights, and to contribute to the solution of the subversion problem. The realm of procedure is after all the judge's special domain; the construction of statutes is a peculiarly judicial art; and the Court's ipse dixit seems more authoritative in these areas than it might if substantive issues of policy were being decided.

Like considerations might seem to have a bearing on another great question in the modern jurisprudence of civil rights—the extent to which the *states* are bound by a federal constitutional standard in their general criminal procedures. But here the problem has been complicated by the Court's respect for a value that ranks very high in the lexicon of some of the judges —the value of federalism. Justice Holmes once said (though not, as it happens, in reference to a procedural issue) that he deprecated the use of the Fourteenth Amendment to prevent experiments "in the insulated chambers afforded by the several States." The modern Court has been troubled by the fear that overly strict constitutional supervision of state law enforcement would impede the evolution of new and more effective methods and would dampen the state's sense of responsibility for policing its own standard.

These misgivings help account for the fact that the Court has advanced more slowly in this field than some libertarians might wish. It will be remembered that by the 1930's the Court had clearly accepted the idea that some procedural rights protected against national action by Amendments IV–VIII, were also protected against state action by the Fourteenth Amendment. The problem then was to determine what those rights were and how they should be applied to limit the states. In 1937 in the *Palko* case Justice Cardozo laid it down that the rights protected were those principles of justice "so rooted in the traditions and conscience of our people as to be ranked as fundamental." Unhappily however this principle, like others that have been encountered in this chronicle, was not quite self-explanatory. Suppose it is decided that the right to counsel is fundamental in the sense intended by the *Palko* doctrine. Does that mean that the right must be granted in every kind of proceeding even down to traffic court cases? Does it mean that the state is obliged to provide counsel for the indigent even in those cases? Or is it necessary, once a right has been identified as worthy of protection, to discriminate between denials of it that are offensive and those that are not?

The modern Court met these difficulties, or attempted to meet them, by developing the "fair trial rule." The right to counsel, for example, *had* been recognized to be protected by the Amendment as long ago as 1932. But, said the Court ten years later, in determining whether a *given* denial of counsel is a denial of due process, we will ask whether "the totality of facts" in the case "constitute a denial of fundamental fairness." Thus an indigent farm laborer was not deprived of due process when the state refused his request to supply counsel in a trial for robbery, because the Supreme Court reading the printed record felt that the trial had been fair.

One trouble with this rule, apart from its possible harshness to the defendant, was its extreme uncertainty. If the totality of facts in a given case was the only basis for determining fairness, it seemed impossible to predict whether a conviction would be upheld unless the predicter could anticipate the thought processes of five members of the Supreme Court. This objection, together with a strong disposition to favor the individual in cases of doubt, led to a series of powerful minority dissents in cases following 1942, and finally in *Adamson* v. *California* (1947) the judges engaged in a full-dress verbal conflict. Justice Black argued eloquently and at length that the Court should take leave of the *Palko* doctrine and its subsidiary, the fair trial rule. Both the intent of the Fourteenth Amendment's framers and considerations of sound judicial policy suggest, he said, that Amendments IV–VIII should be incorporated *in toto* in the Fourteenth. Thus the Court would be deprived of the "boundless power" to expand or contract procedural guarantees; the course of the law would be more certain; and the Court would "extend to all the people of the nation the complete protection of the Bill of Rights."

But Justice Black's assault failed to carry the Court majority. Five members joined in reaffirming the established rules. Justice Frankfurter sharply queried the Black interpretation of the framers' intent, denounced the "incorporation" proposal on the ground that it would imprison the states in eighteenth-century legal concepts, and denied that the *Palko* standard was unduly subjective. On the historical point Frankfurter later received valuable extra-judicial support from Professor Charles

Fairman, whose researches into contemporary documents raised serious doubts that the framers had a clear-cut intention to embody the Bill of Rights in the Amendment. The suggestion that the states should be allowed leeway to experiment with reforms has obvious force, but one's ultimate assessment of it will depend on a judgment of whether the leeway is likely to be used for good or ill. And that judgment in turn is related to the weight that is assigned federalism as a value: does state autonomy work against individual liberty or tend to promote it?

As for the charge of subjectivity, perhaps the best answer is what lawyers call a plea in confession and avoidance. The question of subjectivity versus objectivity is as old as the Supreme Court (in fact, of course, a great deal older). Critics have perennially urged the Court to abolish uncertainties by pronouncing a sweeping rule, but historical experience suggests that such advice is dubious, however well intended. The broadly generalized dogmatism has usually created more mischief than it has cured, both from the Court's own viewpoint and from the viewpoint of public policy. It is reasonable therefore to expect that the rules will emerge gradually as inferences from a multitude of decisions, and to hope that they will be well adapted to reality by the nature of their evolution.

But on the other hand the fair trial rule with its emphasis on the "totality of facts" in each discrete situation seems a barrier to the development of any rule at all, and the Court does have an obligation to make the law as understandable as reality permits. The all-out incorporation principle espoused by Black seems to have provoked a similarly extreme contradictory doctrine. It is not the first time in this history that we have seen wisdom fall between two opposite poles. The list of decisions since 1937 in which procedural rights have been defended against state action is a long one. Here as elsewhere during the modern era the Court has been more vigilant to protect the individual than it was in the past. But it has failed to develop in this field a criterion of decision that seems intellectually defensible or practically tenable.

RACIAL DISCRIMINATION AND THE BOUNDARIES
OF JUDICIAL POWER

In connection with free speech and procedural rights, as we have seen, the modern Court has pursued a somewhat irregular course, alternating between modesty and self-assertion, retreating and advancing by turns. But the third great civil rights problem—racial discrimination—has been handled quite differently. Here the Court has been more venturesome, more confident in announcing its proscriptions. Moreover the doctrinal direction has been consistently (though not unhesitatingly) forward toward a more generous view of the rights of racial minorities and a more daring assessment of the Court's capacity to protect them. And the radical conflicts of opinion among the judges themselves, so frequent in the other cases discussed, have in this field been far less common.

The explanation for this contrast is not hard to guess. With one or two possible exceptions all of the judges appointed to the bench since 1937 shared a general civil rights ethos. Their commitments to it might vary in degree, and the judges might differ in their ideas for implementing it, but they shared it nonetheless. And in that mutual value system the goal of racial equality assumed a special place for several reasons. Partly, no doubt, it was because persecution on the basis of race seemed the most gratuitously evil of totalitarian malignancies. Partly it was because America's primary racial minority, the Negroes, lagged so patently and woefully behind the rest of the nation in their privileges: this problem seemed the greatest because it involved the most glaring injustice. There is usually an arguable justification for restrictions on speech or denial of procedural rights—the state must be defended, the "war against crime" must not be hindered unduly. For racial discrimination there is no such generally commended rationale, but only prejudice. Add to these considerations the fact that Amendments XIV and XV were passed originally to secure Negro rights, though the former amendment had been diverted to other uses. And further add, as has been suggested earlier, that the modern judges were pervasively conscious of America's position as a symbol of the free world and of the new importance of the "non-White" nations in the world arena. The judicial impulse to act forthrightly in this field is easy to understand.

But, however grievous the wrongs and however strong the will to right them, the problems of judicial governance remain problems still. The Court was spared in this field the old self-questioning about whether the challenged state policy was actually justifiable—were the rights of employers to untrammeled economic freedom really superior to the rights of scrubwomen to a living wage? No such baffling calculus need be conducted here, for the side of justice seemed to the Court unarguably manifest. But another question, the sheer issue of judicial power, was not to be similarly bypassed. The authority of the Court is supported (in theory at least) by the force of the national government, and especially the President. But if such support is not accorded, the judiciary's only remaining mainstay is its own prestige. The nation's respect for the judiciary has been great enough, as we have seen, so that the Court can affect policy in marginal ways. It has not usually been so great that the Court can bank on it against a clear-cut and deeply felt political impulse of the majority of the people. In assailing the problem of Negro rights, the Court challenged a significant segment, not a majority, of the nation. But the strain on judicial capacities was not, as it turned out, to be taken lightly.

The modern chapter of the narrative begins in 1938 with *Missouri* v. *Canada*. It will be remembered that the nineteenth-century Court had diminished the possible effect of the Fourteenth Amendment by denying that Congress could reach private persons under the enforcement clause, and by upholding state-required segregation of races (*Civil Rights Cases,* 1883, and *Plessy* v. *Ferguson,* 1896). The first of these doctrines was fairly well supported by the language of the Amendment: "no *State* . . . shall deny to any person . . . the equal protection of the laws." This means, or has meant to the Court, that the Amendment has no bearing on private discriminatory behavior and that Congress' "power to enforce . . . the provisions of this article" extends only to states and to state officials acting under state law. This confining interpretation is not entirely inevitable; Justice Harlan suggested a plausible contrary gloss in his *Civil Rights Cases* dissent. But the Court has never been disposed to follow these suggestions, perhaps feeling that the majority doctrine, whether right or wrong to begin with, was now unshakably established in the constitutional tradition. There seemed then little room for maneuver on this point; private persons could discriminate at will if their own states would tolerate it.

Moreover, as has been remarked earlier, even the states themselves were not seriously embarrassed by the Amendment for some time after *Plessy*'s announcement of the doctrine that the races could be legally separated so long as facilities were equal. The facilities did not have to be *very* equal to pass the Court's mild inspection. However, the "separate but equal" doctrine, even with its dubious acceptance of segregation as a principle, did contain a restrictive potential, in case a libertarian-minded Court should be inclined to turn it into a reality by insisting on true equality.

In the *Missouri* case that note was finally sounded loud and clear. In accordance with the casual standards acceptable in the past, Missouri had never bothered to establish a Negro law school, although it did maintain one limited to whites. Now a Negro student, duly qualified except for his color, sought entrance to this University of Missouri law school and was of course denied. The state argued that there were too few Negro applicants to warrant the setting-up of a special school; and that, pending the day when the number of such applicants would be substantial, Missouri had done its constitutional duty by offering to pay this Negro's tuition at a university in another state. But these evasions, though once serviceable enough, did not impress a Court now coming alive to the problem of civil rights on many fronts. It was held that the right to equality does not "depend upon the number of persons who may be discriminated against," that the discrimination was not excused by its suppositiously "temporary character," and that Missouri could not pass on to some other state its own obligation to provide equality. In short, equal means equal.

The *Missouri* decision signalized a new judicial mood toward Negro rights. It was followed in the next twenty years by the development of an elaborate jurisprudence of equality extending into a large variety of fields. For example, the Court applied the hoary *Cooley* rule to forbid segregation on interstate transportation, this being a subject that required a uniform national rule; and the Interstate Commerce Act was also construed to outlaw segregation. Attempts to discriminate on racial grounds in the real estate field were seriously undermined by the judicial decision that "restrictive covenants" (agreements that a buyer will not resell to Negroes, Jews, etc.) cannot be enforced in state courts, since such enforcement would be "state action" forbidden by the Fourteenth Amendment. Even the enforcement clause of that Amendment was to some extent revitalized by a holding that a state officer who used the power of his office to encroach on an individual's constitutional rights could be punished by federal law (*Screws* v. *United States,* 1945). The Court still adhered to the "state action" limit on the Amendment's range, but it was evidently prepared to interpret that interpretation as generously as reason would allow.

These were important developments; and there were others. But there were two kinds of race discrimination that mattered more than any of the rest: denial of the voting right and denial of adequate education. Inequality in these fields not only deprived the Negro of his present rights, but impaired his chance to improve his lot in the future. And therefore the Court moved in these fields with special determination.

The constitutional problem of voting rights was complicated. The Fifteenth Amendment forbids the states to abridge the right to vote on account of race or color. A state law directly denying Negroes the right would be overthrown as a matter of course, and in 1915 the Court had invalidated a so-called "grandfather clause" which required literacy tests of those who were *not* descendants of those who could vote in 1867. But two difficulties arose. For one thing, the primary was of course the only election that mattered in the one-party South, yet primaries had not been known by the Constitution's framers, and in 1920 the Court had seemed to say that they were, therefore, not elections in the meaning of the Constitution. For another thing, although the state was prohibited by the equal protection clause of the Fourteenth Amendment from excluding Negroes from primaries by law, the Democratic party (a "private" group and therefore untouched by the Amendment) could accomplish the same result by denying them party membership. This indirect abridgment of the voting right was allowed by the Court in a 1935 decision, and the White Primary seemed securely intrenched against Court interference (*Grovey* v. *Townsend*).

But the tide of civil rights sentiment in the country and on the bench could not be checked long by such sophistries. A constitution intended as Story said, to endure for ages, cannot be confined by static definitions that ignore changing realities. In 1941, the Court recognized this, upholding Congress' right to prevent fraud in a primary election for congressional representatives, and conceding that primaries are elections in the constitutional sense. Then in 1944 the White Primary question once more reached the Court (*Smith* v. *Allwright*). Texas had barred Negroes from participation in the Democratic primary by the simple expedient of denying them party membership. Indeed the membership resolution here drawn in question was the same one upheld in 1935. Now, however, the Court was in a different mood, and the recognition that primaries were elections had made the *Grovey* doctrine seem all the more anomalous. The judges therefore held that the action of the party was constitutionally forbidden, because the association between state and party stamped the party's doings as state action:

If the state requires a certain election procedure, prescribes a general election ballot made up of party nominees so chosen and limits the choice of the electorate in general elections for state offices, practically speaking, to those whose names appear on such a ballot, it endorses, adopts and enforces the discrimination against Negroes, practiced by a party entrusted by Texas law with the determination of the qualifications of participants in the primary. This is state action within the meaning of the Fifteenth Amendment.

In other words, the mere fact that the state makes use of the primary results brings the primary procedures within the scope of the Constitution. In the face of this reasoning it became impossible to devise a White Primary arrangement that would not be technically unconstitutional, and the Court made it clear in subsequent decisions that the Fifteenth Amendment "nullifies sophisticated as well as simple-minded modes of discrimination." To be sure, the Court alone could not insure Negroes access to the ballot box; discriminatory administrative practices and the tactics of terror are not always within judicial reach. But the Court had done its part to preserve the idea that the United States is a constitutional democracy.

While these decisions in themselves did not solve the problem of racial disfranchisement, they helped stimulate a movement in that direction, and Negro voting substantially increased in southern states after *Smith* v. *Allwright*. The white Southern reaction was far from joyful of course, but neither was it in general militantly antagonistic to the Court. The truth is that the new doctrine was hard to criticize without challenging the Constitution itself, and the habit of venerating that document was strong. The Constitution does after all enjoin equality in the election process; and no person could rationally deny that the White Primary abridged voting equality. The Constitution and reason were on the judges' side, and these were potent allies.

The Modern Court and Modern America

A similar point can be made concerning *Missouri* v. *Canada* and the question of educational segregation. Not even Justice McReynolds, who dissented in the *Missouri* case, could contend that the state was granting the colored applicant equality of treatment. The best he could offer was his argument that the state had made a "fair effort" to do so. The majority could serenely answer that the Constitution required not efforts but results.

This continued for some time to be the Court's answer. The equality requirement was progressively tightened notch after notch, though segregation itself was not yet queried. In 1950, it was held that Texas had violated the equal protection clause when it denied a Negro entrance to the University of Texas, even though a separate law school for Negroes had been established. The separate school, said the Court unanimously, was not equal to the University of Texas "in those qualities which are incapable of objective measurement but which make for greatness in a law school." By logical extension this opinion certainly condemned all segregation in public professional schools and probably colleges as well. Indeed it can be argued that public school segregation of any kind was inferentially outlawed by the decision. But the Court itself did not draw the inference; it merely decided the instant case. And again, as in the White Primary Case, its position was rationally powerful. For equality *is* constitutionally commanded, and no fair observer could believe that the special Negro school matched the University of Texas.

However, the judges were continually being pressed, by liberal commentators, by counsel, and no doubt by their own consciences, to take the further step of declaring explicitly that segregation per se violated the equal protection clause. And in

1954, they did so, again speaking unanimously. The opinion of Chief Justice Warren was to be, as all members of the Court surely knew, a state paper of enormous importance; inevitably it would be exposed to the most searching criticism. Yet it does not seem in perspective to have been very well thought out. The Chief Justice was forced to admit that the historical intent of the Amendment's framers was inconclusive on the specific question of segregation. He was compelled to reject the contention that the *Plessy* doctrine was currently binding. But he might have made out a strong argument that the framers intended to create an elastic general standard, which could alter and grow with the times; and this argument would help to justify a Court interpretation based on conditions in 1954 rather than 1868. Further, the opinion might have claimed powerful support in precedent both before and after *Plessy*, and thereby undermined in advance the criticism that the decision "was sheer judicial legislation."

Instead the Chief Justice chose to go, almost without preliminary, to the question of whether segregation necessarily involved inequality in contemporary America and to rest his affirmative answer heavily on psychological and sociological literature. If one of the aims of a judicial opinion is to persuade the persuadable, this selection of citations was, to say the least, uninspired. The decision called for the argumentative talents of Marshall and Story rolled into one, and that ideal is rather a lot to hope for. But it is not unfair to wish that the opinion had come a little closer to it.

However, the impact of the opinion, whatever its deficiencies, was not to be mistaken. "Separate facilities are inherently unequal." For the time being the judges postponed any judgment about how the decision should be implemented, but a year later the lower federal courts were ordered to fashion their desegregation decrees in the light of the principles that guide the law of equity (that is, flexibility in the shaping of remedies and due consideration for the problem of adjusting public and private needs). Although this order was obviously designed to permit the states some leeway, the Court was undeviating in its insistence that the states concerned must make "a prompt and reasonable start" toward desegregation and that "the vitality of these constitutional principles cannot be allowed to yield simply because of disagreement with them."

The reaction of the white South to this judicial onslaught on its institutions was noisy and stubborn. Certain "border states," which had formerly maintained segregated school systems, did integrate, and others permitted the token admission of a few Negro students to schools that had once been racially unmixed. However, the Deep South made no moves to obey the judicial command, and in some districts there can be no doubt that the Desegregation decision hardened resistance to integration proposals. The moral support of the President, which might have helped to muster obedience, was accorded too grudgingly and tardily to do much good. The situation settled down into a quasi-stalemate in which the Court steadily reiterated its doctrine as specific cases arose, and the South passionately vowed that it would never yield. The decision had done much good and no doubt some harm. Whether it would ultimately achieve the moral end it contemplated was a question locked, in Justice Story's words, "in the inscrutable purposes of Providence."

The final effect on the judiciary of the decision's backlash is also a matter for conjecture. For the southern foes of the Desegregation doctrine were not content with passive resistance; they mounted a counterattack against the Court. At first the attack was largely rhetorical: the Calhounian slogan of "interposition" was heard in the land once more, with states earnestly proclaiming their sovereignty and impeaching the nation's, as if *Cohens* v. *Virginia* had never been decided and the Civil War never fought. This kind of thing was no cause for perturbation except among those who were already perturbed.

But then, ironically, the Court itself provided an element that made the situation more serious. In 1956 and 1957 it handed down a group of decisions hopefully calculated to moderate the venom of certain "antisubversive" measures. These judicial pronouncements have been touched on earlier in this chapter and their general drift described. They manifestly were not direct challenges of government's power to deal with subversion. The emphasis was on statutory interpretation and procedural caveats throughout. But they furnished the necessary ingredient for an alliance between Southern segregationists and Northerners fearful of domestic subversion and made it possible to shift the attack on the Court from the realm of mere polemics to the much more dangerous arena of Congress. The judgments in the subversive field were catechized as denying the nation the right of self-preservation and Congress the right to function as a co-ordinate branch of government; and the fact that these charges were wildly incongruous with the actual decisions was conveniently ignored. Southerners who frankly favored segregation and Northerners who welcomed a pretext to join them, eagerly supported proposals to "curb" the Court by modifying its appellate jurisdiction.

If the Courts of John Marshall and Morrison R. Waite could have been on hand to observe this development and the twenty-odd years of constitutional history that preceded it, they might well have experienced the shock of recognition. They, too, had been faced by the problem of enforcing a value system that was still a subject of popular controversy. Like the judges of the modern era, they had taken up constitutional clauses of vague and seemingly limited content and had shaped them into the tools of a new jurisprudence. They, too, had struggled to evolve a role for the Court that was adequate to the tasks it faced, yet not beyond its capacities. They, too, had seen the Court assailed and defended for its acts and its failures to act. They, too, were often reminded, as the modern Court has been, that the Constitution's meaning is never quite settled, that the judicial tasks can never be quite done, that the ordeal of self-appraisal is never quite over, and that the challenges to the Court's authority can never quite be stilled. These are the prices that they paid—and the modern judges pay—for maintaining a tribunal that is a vital factor in the American political system.

Epilogue: The Court of Today and the Lessons of History

Those who study history and write about it have always been attracted by the idea that the present is illuminated by the past. No doubt they tend to magnify the virtues of their muse and to expect without warrant that others will heed her. Patterns of error in the very historical record they read should serve to remind them that their mistress is not everyone's fancy and that the present is likely, in large measure, to make up its own mind.

Yet they cannot be entirely dissuaded from hoping that today will learn a little from yesterday, that—to come back without further ado to the subject of this book—the Supreme Court of the 1960's will be understood and evaluated in the light of what has gone before. True, the case for such optimism is not overwhelming. As recently as the New Deal period, we saw that some judges of the Supreme Court itself did not know the history of the bench they occupied, or had failed to understand it. From first to last the Court has been attacked and defended in terms of a historical performance that was often completely fictitious.

The Desegregation decision and the 1956–57 subversion decisions seem to have set going one of those irruptions of anti-judicial spirit that have from time to time enlivened the chronicles of the Court. And as always the attackers have been met and to a degree countered by a muster of ardent champions. In part, as always, this has been a contest between those who happen for the moment to like the Court because it serves their purpose and those who traduce it because it does not. Such clashes by night are not very edifying, but neither are they very novel or alarming. The Court has survived times more perilous than this. An institution that came through the Jeffersonian revolution, the slavery controversy, and the New Deal is not likely to expire in the face of this latter-day threat, noisy though it may be.

However, the clamor has been accompanied by a strain of much more responsible and thoughtful evaluation. The strident voices of the ill-informed or ill-intentioned have awakened others to realize that the case for (or against) judicial review merits serious reconsideration in the light of modern circumstances.

This realization was long overdue. The critical assault on judicial review that culminated in the Battle of 1937, did not destroy the Court, but it did impair many of the ancient myths which had long served as justifications for the Court's activities. Thereafter it was no longer possible for the judges and their supporters to take refuge from reasoned criticism behind the old incantations—the idea that the Court was merely the passive mouthpiece of an unambiguous constitution; the idea that the nature and range of the Court's power to intervene was settled once and for all by the Constitution itself or by unmistakable inferences from the Constitution. There had grown up a generation of jurists and scholars convinced that the Court's judges were conscious molders of policy and that the Constitution had left open many questions about its own meaning, including the question of the Court's proper role.

Presumably judicial review could be defended even in the light of these insights; presumably a viable definition of its role could still be worked out. But evidently this could not be accomplished merely by invoking the discredited mystique of the past. It required a new defense and a new set of definitions that took account of the "new realism" about the Court's nature.

For a good many years after 1937, this need for rethinking was pretty thoroughly ignored both by the judges and by informed students of the Court. The judiciary doled out the "yeas" and "nays" and onlookers viewed with approval or alarm, but there seemed little disposition for either the Court or its critics to go beyond the *ad hoc* issues of the individual cases and find a reasoned apologia for judicial review in the modern era. Finally, when the 1950's were nearly over, the cries of the anguished South and its allies helped inaugurate a current of sober and scholarly discussion. In particular the participants in this discussion have been addressing themselves to a problem framed by the most venerable of modern judges in the words: "when a court should intervene." That is, under what circumstances can the judiciary feel warranted in disallowing the acts of the other branches of government? What are the proper limits of judicial review?

This development is healthy and hopeful. It may end by greatly illuminating the problem of judicial review in modern America. But it does seem fair to say that much of the discussion

Epilogue: The Court of Today

so far, though thoughtful and serious, is marred by inadequate attention to the lessons of history. Of course the Supreme Court of the 1960's must be evaluated as a modern institution, not as an antique. But knowledge of the real (not the fictitious) past of the Court is indispensable to any sound estimate of its capacities in the present and future. The child is father to the man in institutional, as well as individual, life.

In concluding a volume that has compendiously reviewed the history of the Court, it may be useful then to ask what light the chronicle sheds on this contemporary debate. History will not provide final answers to the question of "when a court should intervene" and the other questions that trouble today's judges. But it should carry us a few steps closer to those answers by setting the living problems in a living context.

To begin with, judicial history seems to suggest that this great question of the Court's proper role is not susceptible of any single, final answer. One of the main points to emerge from this study is that the interests and values, and hence the role, of the Court have shifted fundamentally and often in the presence of shifting national conditions. The concept of the judicial function that is reflected in some of Marshall's great opinions after 1815 would not have been appropriate to the Court during Taney's early years. The great Chief Justice was cutting new trails, and the task required the judicious boldness that he so amply possessed. The function of the Taney Court was to preserve and consolidate the imperium Marshall claimed, and the role it played had to be correspondingly modified.

Indeed the facts of the Court's history impellingly suggest a flexible and non-dogmatic institution fully alive to such realities as the drift of public opinion and the distribution of power in the American republic. The comparative meekness of the judiciary during the Civil War years, the retreat in 1937 in the face of the election returns—these are only two dramatic examples of a propensity that has been surprisingly constant. As was suggested in the first chapter of this volume, it is hard to find a single historical instance when the Court has stood firm for very long against a really clear wave of public demand. Even the Income Tax law, popular though it was in some circles, was surely not backed by an imperious popular mandate in the 1890's: a constitutional amendment was not even proposed by Congress until fourteen years after the *Pollock* decision.

This is not to suggest that the historical Court has slavishly counted the public pulse, assessed the power relationships that confronted it, and shaped its decisions accordingly. The process in question is a good deal more subtle than that. We might come closer to the truth if we said that the judges have often agreed with the main current of public sentiment because they were themselves part of that current, and not because they feared to disagree with it.

But the salient fact, whatever the explanation, is that the Court has seldom lagged far behind or forged far ahead of America. And the logic of this, as was also suggested at the outset of this volume, was inherent in the conditions of the Court's inception. Judicial review in its peculiar American form exists because America set up popular sovereignty and fundamental law as twin ideals and left the logical conflict between them unresolved. This dualism gave the Court the opportunity for greatness. But it meant that the opportunity was hedged about by reservations and penalties. A tribunal so conceived was not likely to shape its policies without regard for popular sentiment.

It may be deplorable that this is so. There might be something to be said for a Court that imposed loftier ideals and tried to goad the nation faster toward Utopia. But it is at least very doubtful that such a tribunal could have succeeded in holding the scepter it tried to grasp. The American Supreme Court— it should not be forgotten—is the most powerful court known to history. Foreign observers have never ceased to be amazed at the part played by these nine judges in national affairs, and a multitude of students have sought to account for the judiciary's exalted status in this country. The answer I suggest—illustrated over and over in the historical record we have reviewed—is to be found in what has just been said: that the Court seldom strayed very far from the mainstreams of American life and seldom overestimated its own power resources. To put the thing in a different way, the Court learned to be a political institution and to behave accordingly; and this fact above all accounts for its unique position among the judicial tribunals of the world.

All these observations bear directly on the problem of what role the Court should play, or is likely to play, in the modern American order.

For example, the Court's modern shift away from economic rights and toward civil rights can be properly evaluated only when it is seen in historical perspective. There has been a considerable amount of argument over the question of whether the judges ought to have abandoned their old preoccupation with economic matters, should have turned the property-holder as such over to the legislative power to do with as it wished. Perhaps there are still some marginal issues in this area that are open to fruitful discussion, but surely the broad rejoinder is that history, not the Court, made this decision, as it has made similar decisions in the past. Before 1860, America itself was undecided on the question of nation versus states; before 1932, America was undecided about the question of government economic control versus laissez faire. Until those dates the Court could still play a vital part in helping the nation to make up its mind. It happens that the Court's line in the one case was in accord with the final historical decision, and in the other was not. But this makes little difference to the point. If in either case the Court had tried to follow its old course after the Civil War and the New Deal had respectively signalized firm national judgments, the judges would have been talking to themselves. Ethical justifications for these farewells to the past are no doubt still worth seeking, but we should be clear that they are ex post facto.

As for the modern Court's espousal of civil rights as a substitute for the economic rights it once so cherished, this too was less a matter of deliberate choice than of predictable response to the wave of history. As we have seen, the Court has always tended to focus on the great open questions that plagued America as a whole—the nation-state problem from 1789 to 1860, the business-government problem from 1865 to 1937. To be sure, there are some such "great issues" which are probably not meet for judicial treatment. The slavery question in the 1850's seems in retrospect one of these; the question of foreign policy in modern circumstances is, for rather different reasons, another. But within the limits of what it regards as its capacities, the Court can be expected to preoccupy itself with the issues that most preoccupy America. And civil rights is just such an issue —more important perhaps than any modern American problem except foreign affairs, still undecided in spite of what partisans on either side would like to think, and not by its nature inappropriate for some form of judicial intervention. In turning its attention to this subject, the Court was acting in perfect historical character.

It was to be expected, then, and was, historically speaking,

Epilogue: The Court of Today

"right" that the Court should focus in the modern period on the relationship between government and the individual's rights. But history also has a precept or two to offer in connection with the question of *how* this comparatively new jurisdiction should be administered. What judicial attitudes, what policies, are most likely to serve the cause the judges have so evidently embraced?

In the first place, the record suggests that the principles of this new jurisprudence cannot be reached by a series of leaps and bounds. The Court's great successes in establishing jurisdiction have never been attained that way. We need only recall by way of example the slow and gingerly steps Marshall took from *Marbury* to *Cohens* v. *Virginia* to confirm the Court's supremacy over the states, or the almost painfully gradual accumulation of precedents that led finally to substantive due process in the late nineteenth century. It is in the nature of courts to feel their way along, and it must not be forgotten that this is a court we are speaking of, albeit a most unusual one.

Moreover—it can hardly be said too often—the Supreme Court, being an American institution, is obliged always to reckon with America and her propensities; and America is a nation that moves hesitantly and changes gradually. In spite of our occasional frenzies, the great alterations in the Republic's development have been the result of long experience and slowly growing conviction. There are those on the modern Court—Justices Black and Douglas are the leading exemplars—who would resolve constitutional uncertainties with large, bold, pioneering strokes of the pen. If this is the proper model for judicial governance, then history is indeed an untrustworthy guide.

Rather similar thoughts are aroused when we apply the historical lens to the question that has plagued the modern Court during the past two decades: granting that civil rights are properly within the judicial purview, and granting (at least for argument's sake) that the structure of the new jurisprudence must be built up gradually, how self-assertive should the Court be in imposing the rules it does devise upon the other branches of government? What are the boundaries of modesty on the one hand and "activism" on the other, even in the civil rights field?

Only a rhetorical purpose is served by answering this query in terms that simply ignore the patterns of history. From time to time it is urged that the Court should carry the virtue of modesty to an extreme, adopting a policy of self-restraint that would leave other branches of government almost entirely immune from constitutional restriction. Whatever the theoretical merits of such a suggestion, the short answer is that it asks the Court to take leave of its heritage. The Court of history has never assessed itself so modestly, and there is not much reason to expect that the Court of the future will deliberately choose such a policy of renunciation. In fact we might almost think that the argument in its pure form had been foreclosed by the passage of time. As I have earlier suggested, the process of policy formation in America has been handled by a rough division of labor: representation of immediate and sometimes imperative interests has been assigned to the legislative branch; the judiciary has been bequeathed a significant share of the responsibility for taking the longer view. If the Court, after nearly two centuries, should cease to perform its wonted share of this work, there is grave doubt that the shirked task would get done at all.

And surely American democracy would be poorer. An impulsive nation like ours, much given to short-run fads, enthu-

Epilogue: The Court of Today

siasms and rages, can little afford to dispense with the one governmental element that is disposed by its nature to take the long-run into account. To be sure, the record suggests that these popular passions are usually followed in the fullness of time by a cooling-off phase. The basic tendency of American politics is surely not extremist. But unfortunately these impulses, if not countered, are likely to leave behind them a brood of foolish laws and unfair practices that are harder to disown than they were to adopt. In 1960 the "McCarthyist" spirit seemed to have subsided quite thoroughly as an active political factor. But legislative and administrative remnants of that spirit lived on. America needs the Court's advice and control to help mitigate its own extravagances.

Neither, however, should history be ignored in determining how judicial control should be exercised and when it should be brought to bear. Surely the record teaches that no useful purpose is served when the judges seek all the hottest political caldrons of the moment and dive into the middle of them. Nor is there much to be said for the idea that a judicial policy of flat and uncompromising negation will halt a truly dominant political impulse. Grave though the McCarthyist threat was, a discreet judiciary would not assail every manifestation of it that appeared, or hope to reverse the tide unaided. The Court's greatest successes have been achieved when it has operated near the margins rather than in the center of political controversy, when it has nudged and gently tugged the nation, instead of trying to rule it. Consider the success of the Taney Court in its early years, compromising or skirting the areas of greatest controversy, yet developing on the peripheries of those areas a moderate but real national jurisprudence. Or consider the long campaign on behalf of laissez faire from 1905 to 1934, with its pattern of concessions to the principle of regulation, dotted here and there with a warning that the principle could be carried too far. And compare the Court of these times with that of 1858 or 1938 after the urge to dominate had enjoyed two moments of triumphant ascendancy. The Court ruled more in each case when it tried to rule less, and that paradox is one of the clearest morals to be drawn from this history.

It is true that such a judicial policy calls for rather extraordinary talents of character and intelligence. The Court must alter its own perspectives as history's perspectives are altered, yet must not move so fast that the idea of continuity is lost. It must allow government some leeway to act either wisely or foolishly, yet must not become so acquiescent that the concept of constitutional limit is revealed as an illusion. This requires judges who possess what a great poet called "negative capability"—who can resist the natural human tendency to push an idea to what seems its logical extreme, to have done with half-measures and uncertainties. It requires judges who can practice the arts of discrimination without losing the light of reason and getting lost in a welter of *ad hoc*, pragmatic judgments. For it is part of the glory and strength of the American constitutional tradition that it assumes the possibility of being rational about the state and its powers and limits.

This is a challenging bill of particulars, and the Supreme Court in the modern era has not met it in all respects. The Court has adjusted impressively to a new environment, has embraced a new set of interests and values, has shouldered great new responsibilities in the field of civil rights. But here and there—as in the free speech field—it has oscillated between a doctrine of limit too strict for enforcement and a doctrine of permissiveness that bordered on judicial abdication. Here and there—as in

Epilogue: The Court of Today

the segregation case—it has pressed forward at a rate that seems perilous and perhaps self-defeating. Here and there—as in the cases involving state criminal procedures—it has failed to chart a course that is rationally persuasive or even comprehensible. Here and there—as in the Steel Seizure Case—it has presumed to arbitrate an issue charged with the most explosive and immediate political consequences.

Nevertheless the Court of the modern era, like those of the past, has rendered a service of no small significance. From 1789 to the Civil War, the Court labored to establish a reasoned argument for the cause of union. From the war to 1937 it performed a similar function on behalf of laissez faire. Toward the end of each of those periods, the judges overstepped the practical boundaries of judicial power and endangered the place they had earned in the American governmental system. Since 1937, the Court has striven to evolve a civil rights doctrine that will realize the promise of the American libertarian tradition, yet accord with the imperatives of political reality. Even when criticisms are duly acknowledged, the fact remains that the Court has contributed more to an understanding of this issue than any other agency in American life. It would be a pity if the judges, having done so much, should now once more forget the limits that their own history so compellingly prescribes.

Important Dates

1788 New Hampshire ratifies Constitution
1789 The Republic begins operations
 The Judiciary Act is passed
1791 The Bill of Rights ratified
1793 *Chisholm* v. *Georgia* (states can be sued in the Federal Courts by private citizens of other states)
1798 Eleventh Amendment ratified
 Alien and Sedition Acts
1800 Jefferson elected President
1801 John Marshall appointed Chief Justice
 Judiciary Act of 1801 passed
1802 Judiciary Act of 1801 repealed
1803 *Marbury* v. *Madison*
1805 Impeachment charges against Justice Chase fail
1810 *Fletcher* v. *Peck* (the Yazoo land-grant case)
1811 Justice Story appointed
1816 *Martin* v. *Hunter's Lessee* (state court decisions are reviewable by the Supreme Court)
1819 *McCulloch* v. *Maryland* (the Bank of the United States tax case)
 Dartmouth College v. *Woodward*
1824 *Gibbons* v. *Ogden* (the Steamboat Monopoly case)
1833 *Barron* v. *Baltimore* (the Bill of Rights does not restrict the states)

Important Dates

1835   Death of Marshall

1836   Roger B. Taney appointed Chief Justice

1837   Taney's first term: *Mayor of New York* v. *Miln; Charles River Bridge* v. *Warren Bridge Co.; Briscoe* v. *Bank of Kentucky*

1851   *Cooley* v. *Board of Wardens* (the state can regulate commercial subjects that do not require a uniform national rule—the doctrine of "selective exclusiveness")

1857   *Dred Scott* case (holding the Missouri Compromise invalid)

1862   Justice Samuel F. Miller appointed

1863   Justice Stephen J. Field appointed

1864   Death of Taney
       Chief Justice Salmon P. Chase appointed

1865   Thirteenth Amendment ratified

1866   *Ex Parte Milligan* (invalidating wartime military trial of civilians)

1868   Fourteenth Amendment ratified
       Thomas M. Cooley's *Constitutional Limitations* published

1870   Fifteenth Amendment ratified
       Hepburn v. *Griswold* (invalidating the Legal Tender Act in certain respects)

1871   *Legal Tender Cases* (upholding the Legal Tender Act in all respects)

1873   *Slaughterhouse Cases* (the Fourteenth Amendment does not forbid a state-granted monopoly)

1874   Chief Justice Morrison R. Waite appointed

1877   *Munn* v. *Illinois* (rate regulation of grain elevator rates by state is not forbidden by the Fourteenth Amendment)

1888   Chief Justice Melville W. Fuller appointed

1890   Minnesota Commission case (state rate regulation without judicial review denies due process)

1895   *United States* v. *E. C. Knight Co.* (the Sherman Antitrust Act cannot constitutionally apply to monopolies in manufacturing)
       Pollock v. *Farmers' Loan and Trust Co.* (the Income Tax case)

1896   *Plessy* v. *Ferguson* (the state may require separate facilities for different races providing that the facilities are equal—the "separate but equal doctrine")

233

1902   Justice Oliver Wendell Holmes appointed

1904   *McCray* v. *United States* (the Oleomargarine Tax case)

1905   *Lochner* v. *New York* (the Fourteenth Amendment forbids general hours regulation)

      Swift and Co. v. *United States* (the Antitrust Act can validly apply to sales monopolies)

1910   Chief Justice Edward D. White appointed

1913   Sixteenth Amendment ratified

1916   Justice Louis D. Brandeis appointed

1918   *Hammer* v. *Dagenhart* (the Child Labor case)

1919   *Schenck* v. *United States* (the "clear and present danger" rule)

1921   Chief Justice William H. Taft appointed

1923   *Adkins* v. *Children's Hospital* (the Washington, D.C., Minimum Wage case)

1934   *Nebbia* v. *New York* (upholding the validity of a state milk control law)

1935   *Schechter Poultry Corp.* v. *United States* (holding the National Industrial Recovery Act unconstitutional)

1936   *United States* v. *Butler* (holding the Agricultural Adjustment Act unconstitutional)

      Carter v. *Carter Coal Co.* (holding the Bituminous Coal Act unconstitutional)

      Morehead v. *Tipaldo* (holding the New York Minimum Wage Law unconstitutional)

      Franklin D. Roosevelt re-elected

1937   The "court-packing" plan submitted to Congress, February 5

      West Coast Hotel v. *Parrish* (upholding the Minimum Wage Law of the State of Washington), March 29

      The National Labor Relations Act decisions (upholding the N.L.R.A.), April 12

      Steward Machine Co. v. *Davis* (upholding the Social Security Act), May 24

      Justice Willis Van Devanter retires, June 2

      Justice Hugo L. Black appointed, August 17

1941   Justice Harlan F. Stone appointed Chief Justice

      United States v. *Darby Lumber Co.* (upholding the Fair Labor Standards Act)

Important Dates

1944 *Smith* v. *Allwright* (the White Primary case)

1946 Chief Justice Fred M. Vinson appointed

1947 *Adamson* v. *California* (affirming that the procedural protections of the Bill of Rights are not embodied in the Fourteenth Amendment)

1951 *Dennis* v. *United States* (upholding convictions of Communist party leaders under the Smith Act of 1940)

1952 *Youngstown Co.* v. *Sawyer* (the Steel Seizure case)

1953 Chief Justice Earl Warren appointed

1954 *Brown* v. *Board of Education* (the Public School Desegregation case)

1955 *Brown* v. *Board of Education* (the enforcement decision)

1956 *Pennsylvania* v. *Nelson* (invalidating state sedition laws)

Bibliographical Essay

The body of literature pertaining to the Supreme Court of the United States and to American constitutional law is enormous. Leaving aside such ancient subjects as theology which have been accumulating their bibliographies for centuries, and such modern subjects as physical science which receive infusions from numberless scholarly sources all over the globe, there are probably few areas of human knowledge that have consumed more printers' ink than this one. Certainly it is hard to think of a modern subject that is more elaborately indexed and annotated. And the scholarly standard of most of this literature has been very high. Partly perhaps because of the immediately practical and sometimes very important implications of the subject, a noble tradition of precision and thoroughness has usually been maintained. When several million dollars or a human life hinge on the answer to a scholarly question, the sinfulness of loose thinking and careless documentation is forcefully underlined.

However, this virtue has its defect, which takes the form of an abiding reluctance to generalize or to carry inquiry beyond the borders of the technical legal issue into the realms of philosophy or interpretive history. The result is that, while the literature abounds with dependable expositions and critiques of special doctrinal problems, there is surprisingly little general analysis of the Supreme Court's place in American life, or evaluation of the Court's work in a framework wider than that of today's—or tomorrow's—

litigation. There are notable exceptions of course, some of which will be mentioned below. But the general situation is as described, and it has no doubt helped to foster the quite erroneous idea that the material of American constitutional law is, for the non-lawyer, either impossibly recondite or impossibly dull, and probably both.

Even a brief foray into the actual opinions of the Supreme Court will usually be enough to dispel these notions. The reports of these opinions are the great primary source for those who would dip further than a book like the present one goes into the Court's doings. They appear in three equally authoritative editions—the *United States Reports,* which is the official publication of the government; and the *Lawyer's Edition* and the *Supreme Court Reporter,* which are privately published. They differ somewhat in the amount and kind of scholarly material they provide to aid the student who uses them, but all three print the Court opinions in full. They are cited by the way in legal publications by volume, abbreviated name, and page in that order; e.g., 325 U.S. 1 means volume 325 of the *United States Reports,* page one. This is the standard citation form used in referring to journals as well, and journal articles will be so cited in this bibliographical note. Until 1875, the official reports were identified by the name of the reporter (e.g., 7 *Wallace* 700). This practice was abandoned with the ninety-first volume, and thereafter the official citation is the one just illustrated.

Second only to the reports themselves are the commentaries on and annotations of the Constitution, which have been produced by scholars throughout the Republic's history. The first and most significant is the *Federalist Papers,* written by Madison, Hamilton, and Jay during the ratification controversy. The authors were explaining what the Constitution *would* mean if it were ratified, and their explanations were sometimes clouded by the uncertainties that always afflict prophets and sometimes colored by the zeal of the authors to gain acceptance for the document two of them had helped to compose. But in general they guessed remarkably well, and the *Federalist* was much used as a guide by early judges, especially Marshall, when they pronounced the doctrines that have made our constitutional system what it is. Certain later commentaries have also served this dual function of both describing and influencing the nature of American constitutional law. James Kent's

Commentaries on American Law (4 vols., 1830) and Joseph Story's *Commentaries on the Constitution of the United States* (3 vols., 1833) affected constitutional development for many years and are still worth consulting, both as guides and as historically important documents. Thomas M. Cooley's *Treatise on the Constitutional Limitations Which Rest upon the Legislative Power of the States of the American Union* (1868) has similar attributes. It played a decisive part in shaping the doctrines of constitutional laissez faire that were so important to our public law until 1937.

The nearest modern equivalent to these salient works is Edward S. Corwin's herculean *Constitution of the United States of America* (1953), which he edited as an official publication of the national government. Professor Corwin's name will recur over and over in this bibliographical note, for he is without any serious competitor the foremost living scholar in the field, and he has imbedded in this work the accumulated knowledge and insight of a lifetime. His much smaller volume, *The Constitution and What It Means Today* (1958) is also very useful for those who want a brief, historically grounded elucidation of particular clauses of the Constitution.

Another major lode of great richness is the scholarly journals— the law reviews and the periodicals devoted to history and political science. It would serve no purpose to list these numerous journals individually. Particular articles which I have found especially important or helpful will be referred to below. At this point it is enough to draw the reader's attention to the *indexes* that will help him chart his way through this sea of periodical literature to the subject he seeks. The *Index to Legal Periodicals* covers the law reviews; the *Reader's Guide to Periodical Literature*, the *International Index*, and *Public Affairs Information Service* blanket the rest of the field pretty thoroughly. Each of these publications provides a comprehensive subject index, as well as other reference keys. *P.A.I.S.* has the virtue of listing books as well as periodical articles.

Casebooks (i.e., abridged selections of leading decisions) also deserve brief mention, for the cases are the heart of the subject matter. No historical subject can be studied very fruitfully without some acquaintance with original sources, and this is emphatically true of American constitutional history, which has been so

Bibliographical Essay

heavily determined by what judges had to say in specific cases. And, although the *reports* are, as I have said, worth knowing in their pristine form, a carefully chosen and edited casebook can help the reader understand the context of the subject and direct him to the mileposts along the way. There are many casebooks to choose from, but most of them are published for use in law school classes by fledgling lawyers, and these are likely to omit cases of historical importance which are no longer binding as precedent (e.g., the *Dred Scott* case or the Income Tax decision of 1895). Lawrence B. Evans, *Cases on American Constitutional Law* (1952) is one that gives history its due; John P. Frank, *Cases and Materials on Constitutional Law* (1952), and Walter F. Dodd, *Cases and Materials on Constitutional Law* (1954) are two others. Two valuable books which include historically oriented introductory essays to the several chapters are Alpheus T. Mason and William M. Beaney, *American Constitutional Law* (1959) and Wallace Mendelson, *The Constitution and the Supreme Court* (1959). Robert E. Cushman, *Leading Constitutional Decisions* (1958) and Charles Fairman, *American Constitutional Decisions* (1948) are rather briefer volumes than those so far mentioned and tend to be organized analytically rather than historically, but they both provide extremely helpful and sometimes brilliant annotations of the cases they include and the developments they record. Certain special selections of cases and materials also deserve mention, among them Thomas I. Emerson and David Haber, *Political and Civil Rights in the United States* (1952), Zechariah Chafee, *Documents on Fundamental Human Rights* (1952), and Mark de W. Howe, *Cases on Church and State in the United States* (1952)

There are a number of generalized treatments of American constitutional history, and the greatest of these is surely Charles Warren, *The Supreme Court in United States History* (2 vols., 1925). It is not a full history of American constitutional law but rather of the Court as an institution; it carries the reader only to 1918; and some may feel that it is marred by excessive pro-judicialism. Yet it is one of the most interesting and valuable achievements in the field to date. Carl B. Swisher, *American Constitutional Development* (1954) and Alfred H. Kelly and W. A. Harbison, *The American Constitution* (1955) are useful and up-to-date histories which deal with constitutional development in its broadest sense, not merely (as does the present volume) with the Supreme Court's contributions to the subject.

It is important for the reader to be reminded that constitutional law has been made by presidents, congresses, custom, and other agencies, as well as by the courts. Andrew C. McLaughlin, *A Constitutional History of the United States* (1935) is similarly broad in scope and a very stimulating account as far as it goes, but it thins out after the 1880's and stops short in 1932. Homer C. Hockett, *The Constitutional History of the United States* (2 vols., 1939) is a rather pedestrian study and concludes with 1876, but the student will sometimes find there substantial accounts of particular subjects that may be treated more briefly in the histories that conceive their assignment in more sophisticated terms. Benjamin F. Wright, *The Growth of American Constitutional Law* (1942) restricts itself to the history of judicial review but provides a remarkably thorough and condensed treatment of that subject together with a number of valuable critical insights. Louis Boudin, *Government by Judiciary* (2 vols., 1932) and William W. Crosskey, *Politics and the Constitution in the History of the United States* (2 vols., 1953) are special cases. Both authors have drawn exhaustively on original sources; their books are always provocative and here and there brilliantly perceptive; Crosskey's is especially distinguished for its documentation and close argument. Yet each suffers from the insuperable handicap that it rests on an unsustainable thesis—Boudin that the Court has been the consistent and wilful tool of capitalism, Crosskey that the Constitution was intended by the framers to establish a unitary national system of government with no regard to states' rights.

In addition to these comprehensive histories, the reader seeking a general understanding of the Court and the Constitution in American life can be referred to a small but distinguished company of evaluative essays. James B. Thayer, "The Origin and Scope of the American Doctrine of Constitutional Law," 7 *Harvard Law Review* 129 (1893) is dedicated to the proposition that the Court should only overturn legislative acts when they are invalid beyond "rational question," and this view has undoubtedly influenced generations of judges and critics. Max Lerner, "The Supreme Court and American Capitalism," 42 *Yale Law Journal* 668 (1933) persuasively relates the historical swings in court doctrine to changes in the nature of American capitalistic enterprise. Thomas R. Powell, "The Logic and Rhetoric of Constitutional Law," 15 *Journal of Philosophy, Psychology and Scientific Method* 654 (1918) is a penetrating analysis of the judicial process by one of the great scholars in the field. These essays are also available in Robert G. McCloskey (ed.), *Essays in Constitutional Law* (1957), a volume which contains several other short treatments of constitutional subjects.

Benjamin N. Cardozo, *The Nature of the Judicial Process* (1921), though by no means limited to constitutional jurisprudence, is enlightening to a student of the Supreme Court. The author himself was to become one of the Court's most revered members. Another great judge, Learned Hand, reflects on the role of courts, including the Supreme Court, in *The Bill of Rights* (1958); and yet another very brilliant one, Robert H. Jackson, sets forth his notions in *The Supreme Court in the American System of Government* (1955). These last two volumes are particularly relevant for the student who is concerned with the modern Court's inner conflict over "activism" or "self-restraint" (two perhaps overworn terms, which are nevertheless convenient shorthand for the problem discussed in the later chapters of this book). The authors must be classified as rather extreme proponents of the self-denying concept of the judicial function. Another judge-authored book of interest is Charles E. Hughes, *The Supreme Court of the United States* (1928). Hughes was to serve, of course, as Chief Justice of the Court during one of its stormiest periods, and the volume is thus significant as a document as well as a description. Although the author does concede that the Court has sometimes erred, his sentiments are heavily and sometimes uncritically pro-judicial. Charles P. Curtis, *Lions under the Throne* (1947) is a witty and informed general treatment of the Court, which should be both comprehensible and interesting to the lay reader. Robert K. Carr, *The Supreme Court and Judicial Review* (1942) is a concise and intelligent survey of the main problems raised by America's peculiar institution. Edward S. Corwin, "The Higher Law Background of American Constitutional Law," 42 *Harvard Law Review*, 149, 365 (1928) goes farther than any other single work I know to explain how the curious institution of judicial review came into being in

America. Several of the essays mentioned in this paragraph and the one preceding will be found in the massive compilation by the Association of American Law Schools, *Selected Essays in Constitutional Law* (4 vols., 1938), which is a goldmine of great expanse and value. A supplementary volume covering the period since 1938 is devoutly to be wished.

In addition to such general works treating the Constitution as a whole, there are a large number of specific studies dealing with the history of particular constitutional and judicial subjects. Among those of special relevance to matters emphasized in this volume is the standard and masterful treatment of constitutional and other questions raised by the American presidency, Edward S. Corwin's, *The President: Office and Powers* (1957). Andrew C. McLaughlin, *The Courts, the Constitution, and Parties* (1912) is still the best work on the party system and the American Constitution. It would be very useful if someone could carry the story forward to the present. Benjamin F. Wright, *The Contract Clause of the Constitution* (1938) is the ablest and most thorough treatment of that one-time pillar of American constitutional law. The commerce clause is dealt with in many studies, the best of which are Edward S. Corwin, *Commerce Power versus States Rights* (1936) and Robert L. Stern, "The Commerce Clause and the National Economy, 1933–1946," 59 *Harvard Law Review*, 645, 883 (1946). Both of these concentrate a good deal on the fairly recent past; there is not, so far as I know, a good, full-scale treatment of the clause's history from the beginning. Charles Fairman, *The Law of Martial Rule* (1930) is instructive in connection with this chronic problem of constitutional government. Felix Frankfurter and J. M. Landis, *The Business of the Supreme Court* (1928) is the standard work on the history of the Court's jurisdiction. Charles Warren's *History of the American Bar* (1912) provides valuable background material for an understanding of the Court and its achievements, and his classic article, "Legislative and Judicial Attacks on the Supreme Court of the United States," 47 *American Law Review* 1 (1913) is a condensed account of some of the slings and arrows the Court has suffered in its history.

Several of the general works already mentioned shed light on the eternally vexing question of what the Constitution was intended to mean by those who framed and ratified it. Max Farrand,

Bibliographical Essay

The Records of the Federal Convention of 1787 (4 vols., 1911, 1937) and Jonathon Elliott, *The Debates in the Several State Conventions on the Adoption of the Federal Constitution* (5 vols., 1836) are indispensable. Charles A. Beard, *An Economic Interpretation of the Constitution* (1949) and Charles Warren, *The Making of the Constitution* (1937) are largely concerned with the broad motivations of the Founding Fathers, the first contending by powerful implication that the Constitution was designed to serve the economic interests of those who composed and sponsored it, the second attributing rather nobler instincts to these early "Federalists." This much controverted question is relevant to the present volume only insofar as an answer to it might illuminate later problems of constitutional exegesis. Unfortunately such answers as have been arrived at leave wide margins of uncertainty, and a reader is led to feel that the framers' motives were as mixed and ambiguous as their language often was and can furnish no very reliable clue to the meaning of specific clauses. In any case, it should be borne in mind that Beard's interpretation has been profoundly criticized, the most recent assaults being mounted by Robert E. Brown, *Charles Beard and the Constitution* (1956), and by Forrest McDonald, *We the People: The Economic Origins of the Constitution* (1958).

As for the question of the Constitution's intent with respect to the Supreme Court's powers, a great deal has been written. Charles A. Beard, *The Supreme Court and the Constitution* (1912) and Brinton Coxe, *Judicial Power and Unconstitutional Legislation* (1893) are old, standard works supporting the view that the framers had the plain intention to vest the Court with full power to review both the acts of states and of Congress. Edward S. Corwin, *The Doctrine of Judicial Review* (1914) gravely undermined Beard's evidence, and a number of other scholars have made it abundantly clear that, though the framers did expect to see judicial review exercised in some form, few of them had a clear understanding of judicial review in the extent and form that ultimately developed.

For the period of Court history extending from 1789 to 1835, some of the general works already cited are particularly useful, especially Warren's *The Supreme Court in United States History*. Apart from these, the two most broadly informative secondary sources are Charles G. Haines, *The Role of the Supreme Court in American Government and Politics, 1789–1835* (1944) and Albert J. Beveridge, *The Life of John Marshall* (4 vols., 1916). The first is the most detailed history of the period and is written from an Antifederalist viewpoint. The second is almost idolatrous toward Marshall but is surely one of the best biographies of an American statesman yet produced and is at the same time a fascinating history of the Court and the Constitution during the "great Chief Justice's" lifetime. Charles Warren, "New Light on the History of the Federal Judiciary Act of 1789," 37 *Harvard Law Review* 49 (1923) is an essay of considerable importance, for it encouraged the Supreme Court of the 1930's to reinterpret doctrines which had endured for a century (*Erie R.R. Co.* v. *Tompkins*, 304 U.S. 64 [1938]). Edward S. Corwin, *The Doctrine of Judicial Review* (1914) contains the best essay on *Marbury* v. *Madison*, and his *John Marshall and Constitution* (1919) is an excellent short treatment of Marshall's work. Felix Frankfurter, *The Commerce Clause under Marshall, Taney and Waite* (1937) provides an insightful commentary on the development of this doctrine in the Marshall era. On the perennial problem of the Court's role in relation to the other branches of government, both Charles Warren, *Congress, the Constitution, and the Supreme Court* (1925) and James B. Thayer, "The Origin and Scope of the American Doctrine of Constitutional Law" deserve mention. No biography of a judge of the period compares in scope with Beveridge's work on Marshall, but Donald G. Morgan, *Justice William Johnson* (1954), John T. Horton, *James Kent: A Study in Conservatism* (1939), and W. W. Story, ed., *Life and Letters of Joseph Story* (2 vols., 1951) contain useful material.

On the Taney regime (1836–64) the most thorough secondary work is Charles G. Haines and Foster H. Sherwood, *The Role of the Supreme Court in American Government and Politics, 1835–1864* (1957). This volume contains a wealth of material, but it is not as well-ordered or penetrating as the senior author's earlier work on the preceding constitutional period. The most useful judicial biography of the era is Carl B. Swisher, *Roger B. Taney* (1935). Francis P. Weisenburger, *The Life of John McLean: A Politician on the Supreme Court* (1937) is also enlightening. Richard P. Longaker, "Andrew Jackson and the Judiciary," 71 *Political*

Bibliographical Essay

Science Quarterly 341 (1956) is a useful paper. Elizabeth K. Bauer, *Commentaries on the Constitution, 1790–1860* (1952) is worth consulting for the light it throws on the controversy between nationalist and states' rights interpretations of the Constitution. The best single work on the *Dred Scott* case is Edward S. Corwin's essay, contained in *The Doctrine of Judicial Review* (1914). His essay, "The Doctrine of Due Process before the Civil War," 24 *Harvard Law Review* 366 (1911) is also indispensable for understanding both this constitutional era and the one that followed it. James G. Randall, *Constitutional Problems under Lincoln* (1951) is by far the most complete account of that subject.

On the constitutional problems of the Civil War and its aftermath, Charles Fairman's work is outstanding. His *Mr. Justice Miller and the Supreme Court, 1862–1890* (1939) is rich in historical background as well as in understanding of one of the era's most influential jurists. His *Law of Martial Rule* cited above contains reliable accounts and evaluations of such decisions as *Vallandigham* and *Milligan.* Some background on both will also be found in Wood Gray, *The Hidden Civil War: The Story of the Copperheads* (1942). Samuel Klaus, *The Milligan Case* (1929) provides ample documentary material on the *Milligan* decision, including arguments of counsel. Fairman's "Mr. Justice Bradley's Appointment to the Supreme Court and the Legal Tender Cases," 54 *Harvard Law Review* 977, 1128 (1941) contains an analysis of the charge that Grant "packed" the Court to insure a judgment favorable to the Republican policy and is perhaps the most thorough study yet made of the process by which a Supreme Court judge is appointed. Carl B. Swisher, *Stephen J. Field, Craftsman of the Law* (1930) is also valuable in connection with these cases, as well as for its treatment of the constitutional period (1863–97) during which Field occupied, and influenced, the bench.

The inception and purpose of the "war amendments" (XIII, XIV, XV) have interested generations of constitutional scholars, and the problems are still very lively because these amendments, particularly the Fourteenth, play such an important part in modern constitutional jurisprudence. On the question of whether that amendment was designed to protect business as it ultimately did, see Howard J. Graham, "The Conspiracy Theory of the Fourteenth Amendment," 47 *Yale Law Journal* 371 (1938) which pretty well disposes of the idea that the framers set out to shelter corporations by anticipating that the word "person" would be interpreted to embrace them. For an instructive account of how that idea got started, see Andrew C. McLaughlin, "The Court, the Corporation, and Conkling," 46 *American Historical Review* 45 (1940). On the general question of the Amendment's intent, see Horace B. Flack, *Adoption of the Fourteenth Amendment* (1908), Joseph B. James, *The Framing of the Fourteenth Amendment* (1956) and Benjamin B. Kendrick, *Journal of the Joint Committee of Fifteen on Reconstruction* (1914). Flack seeks to support the view that the framers intended to apply the Bill of Rights to the states by way of the Fourteenth Amendment. Charles Fairman and Stanley Morrison, "Does the Fourteenth Amendment Incorporate the Bill of Rights?" 2 *Stanford Law Review* 5 (1949) effectively challenged this contention on the basis of hitherto unexamined evidence. James recovered some, not all, of the lost ground in the book just cited.

On the question of whether the "equal protection" clause was designed to outlaw all types of racial discrimination, including educational, see John P. Frank and Robert F. Munro, "The Original Understanding of Equal Protection of the Laws," 50 *Columbia Law Review* 131 (1950); and Jacobus tenBroek, *Anti-Slavery Origins of the Fourteenth Amendment* (1951). Both these works contend strongly for an antisegregationist view of the clause, based on the explicit intentions of those who composed it. But I find more persuasive the argument of Alexander M. Bickel, "The Original Understanding and the Segregation Decision," 69 *Harvard Law Review* 1 (1955) that the framers, being unable to settle the question one way or another, passed on a kind of blank check to posterity.

With the growing movement for the welfare state in the early twentieth century, Americans became sharply aware that the Supreme Court's laissez faire doctrines were a formidable roadblock, and scholarly attention was focused on the question of how that obstacle came into being. The evolution of the due process, commerce, and tax clauses in the late nineteenth century was exposed to very close, and often critical, examination. Only a few of the many works on these matters can be cited here. Benjamin R. Twiss, *Lawyers and the Constitution* (1942) is a good treatment, particularly enlightening because it illustrates the great part eminent counsel can play in providing the Court ideas and supporting arguments. Edward S. Corwin, *The Twilight of the Supreme Court* (1934) brilliantly analyzes the pre-1900 background of the doctrines, as well as their development in later years. His *Court over Constitution* (1938) contains the best short essay on the Income Tax decision of 1895, and a penetrating discussion of the contrast between judicial review as originally conceived and judicial review in its modern incarnation.

On the commerce clause in this era, Corwin's *Commerce Power versus States' Rights* (1936) and Robert L. Stern, "That Commerce Which Concerns More States Than One," 47 *Harvard Law Review* 1375 (1934) are particularly valuable. Isaiah L. Sharfman's magisterial study, *The Interstate Commerce Commission* (5 vols., 1931–37), treats, among many other things, the constitutional vicissitudes of that important regulatory agency. For the constitutional difficulties faced by the American regulatory movement as a whole, see Merle Fainsod and Lincoln Gordon, *Government and the American Economy* (1948).

The development of modern due process is treated at length in most of the general histories mentioned earlier. Rodney L. Mott, *Due Process of Law* (1926) is a thorough but not very stimulating account of the matter. Perhaps the most satisfying short essay is Walton H. Hamilton's "The Path of Due Process of Law" in *The Constitution Reconsidered*, edited by Conyers Read (1938). The rubric of "business affected with a public interest," that specialized variant of due process doctrine, attracted a great deal of scholarly attention in its heyday, and among the most illuminating essays about it are: Maurice Finkelstein, "From *Munn* v. *Illinois* to *Tyson* v. *Banton*: A Study in the Judicial Process," 27 *Columbia Law Review* 769 (1927) and Breck P. McAllister, "Lord Hale and Business Affected with a Public Interest," 43 *Harvard Law Review* 759 (1930).

The years 1900–1937, beginning as they did with the rise of the Progressive Movement and culminating in the constitutional crisis evoked by the New Deal, have been studied very intensively by both contemporaneous and later scholars. Most of Professor Corwin's books already mentioned are relevant, indeed indispensable, to an understanding of this era. The other great critical scholar of Corwin's generation was Thomas R. Powell, and his almost innumerable articles can be consulted *passim* for their pitilessly mordant exposure of the Court's logical and rhetorical deficiencies. "The Judiciality of Minimum Wage Legislation," 37 *Harvard Law Review* 545 (1924) on the *Adkins* case; "Commerce, Pensions and Codes," 49 *Harvard Law Review* 1, 193 (1935) on the judicial reaction to the New Deal; and "The Supreme Court and State Police Power, 1922–30," 18 *Virginia Law Review* (1931–32) are examples only. A full bibliography of his work would be practically a history of the constitutional era, and it would be a service to scholarship if at least a substantial selection of his papers could be brought together and published in book form.

Biographies of judges who served on the Court during this period are often useful for the light they cast on the history of the times as well as on the character of the judicial process. A full-scale biography of Justice Holmes has not yet been done, but Max Lerner, *The Mind and Faith of Justice Holmes* (1948) is a well-chosen selection of Holmes' own writings and contains excellent introductory material. Felix Frankfurter, *Mr. Justice Holmes and the Supreme Court* (1939) is a brief but revealing essay. Incidentally it includes an appendix listing and briefly describing decisions holding state actions invalid under the Fourteenth Amendment. Alpheus T. Mason, *Brandeis—A Free Man's Life* (1946) and *Harlan Fiske Stone, Pillar of the Law* (1956) are very useful. The latter volume, which draws extensively on Stone's private papers, provides the most intimate picture of the Court in action that has yet been put on paper. It is particularly valuable for an understanding of the Court fight of 1937, although some of the author's evaluations have been queried by other observers and participants. Merlo J. Pusey, *Charles Evans Hughes* (1951) is also valuable, and some of its judgments are at variance with those of Professor Mason. Joel F. Paschal, *Mr. Justice Sutherland* (1951) is a good starting point for understanding the conservative jurisprudence against which Stone so forcefully argued.

On the due process clause during this period, Virginia Wood, *Due Process of Law—1932–1949* (1951) provides useful background. On the commerce clause, Corwin's *Commerce Power versus States' Rights* is again relevant, and Robert L. Stern, "The Commerce Clause and the National Economy," 59 *Harvard Law Review* 645, 883 (1946) is a condensed and well-organized treatment of doctrine both before and after 1937. Robert G. Cushman, "Social and Economic Controls through Federal Taxation," 18 *Minnesota Law Review* 759 (1934) is a good treatment of that important issue. Louis L. Jaffe, "An Essay on Delegation of Legislative Power," 47 *Columbia Law Review* 359, 561 (1947) is the best thing I know on that subject.

The fight over the Court-packing plan is of course an important chapter in the history of the New Deal, and material relevant to it will be found in most of the vast number of memoirs and histories that are currently pouring forth as well as in many of the general works and biographies already cited. Robert H. Jackson, *The Struggle for Judicial Supremacy* (1941) is especially useful. Joseph W. Alsop and Turner Catledge, *The 168 Days* (1938) is a popular blow-by-blow account of the political struggle waged by the Roosevelt administration and its opponents.

The development of the Fourteenth Amendment as a protection for liberty of expression and other civil rights is recorded in Charles Warren, "The New Liberty under the Fourteenth Amendment," 39 *Harvard Law Review* 431 (1926), as well as in many general works. Zechariah Chafee, *Free Speech in the United States* (1948) is a fascinating account and analysis of doctrines in this field by the man who probably contributed more to the field's development than any other non-judicial figure.

On the general pattern of constitutional development since 1937, see Edward S. Corwin, *Constitutional Revolution Ltd.* (1941); Charles H. Pritchett, *The Roosevelt Court* (1948) and *Civil Liberties and the Vinson Court* (1954) and Bernard Schwartz, *The Supreme Court: Constitutional Revolution in Retrospect* (1957), as well of course as the general histories cited previously. The nature of the modern relationship between the nation and the states is trenchantly analyzed in Edward S. Corwin, "The Passing of Dual Federalism," 36 *Virginia Law Review* 1 (1950). Robert L. Stern, "The Problems of Yesteryear—Commerce and Due Process," 4 *Vanderbilt Law Review* 446 (1951) is the most succinct statement of the modern status of these once formidable constitutional problems. His "The Commerce Clause and the National Economy," previously cited, is an authoritative treatment of the commerce clause in particular during these years. On the old but still lively question of the relation between the commerce clause and state power, see Noel T. Dowling, "Interstate Commerce and State Power," 47 *Columbia Law Review* 547 (1947). The best things I know on the executive power and the Steel Seizure incident are Edward S. Corwin, "The Steel Seizure Case: A Judicial Brick without Straw," 53 *Columbia Law Review* 53 (1953) and Paul G. Kauper, "The Steel Seizure Case: Congress, the President and the Supreme Court," 51 *Michigan Law Review* 141 (1952). The problem of labor picketing and other union activity as a "constitutional right" is dealt with in Charles O. Gregory, *Labor and the Law* (1949); Archibald Cox, "Strikes, Picketing, and the Constitution," 4 *Vanderbilt Law Review* (1951) makes the most promising suggestion I have seen for reconciling the logical and practical difficulties inherent in this problem. Arthur E. Sutherland, "Restricting the Treaty Power," 65 *Harvard Law Review* 1305 (1952) is a good condensed summary of the constitutional problems raised by the power to make international agreements, and an evaluation of the proposals that have been made to circumscribe that authority.

Three informative and provocative essays on modern free speech doctrine are Wallace Mendelson, "Clear and Present Danger—from Schenck to Dennis," 52 *Columbia Law Review* 313 (1952); Nathaniel L. Nathanson, "The Communist Trial and the Clear and Present Danger Test," 63 *Harvard Law Review* 1167 (1950); and Edward S. Corwin, "Bowing out 'Clear and Present Danger,'" 27 *Notre Dame Law Review* 329 (1952). Zechariah Chafee, *Free Speech in the United States* and other general works cited above, are also useful. These books should also be referred to for treatments of free religious expression, which raises some judicial problems that are distinguishable from the problems posed by political speech. One of the best essays on the general problem of civil liberties and the modern Court is Paul A. Freund's "Concord and Discord," in his *On Understanding the Supreme Court* (1949).

The issue of state aid to religion has evoked a volume of literature which is perhaps disproportionate to its importance. Leo Pfeffer, *Church, State, and Freedom* (1953) is the most thorough defense of the Court's sometime doctrine that the state must not aid religion in any form. James M. O'Neill, *Religion and Education under the Constitution* (1949); Edward S. Corwin, "The Supreme

Court as National School Board," 14 *Law and Contemporary Problems* 3 (1949); and John C. Murray, "Law or Prepossessions?" 14 *Law and Contemporary Problems* 23 (1949), all come down heavily on the other side. The difficulty in this field, as in so many other fields of constitutional controversy, is that the contestants are more convincing when they criticize their opponents' interpretations than when they seek to establish the validity of their own; and this comment applies to both sides in this controversy.

The question of procedural rights is dealt with broadly but thoroughly by David Fellman, *The Defendant's Rights* (1958). William M. Beaney, *The Right to Counsel in American Courts* (1955) is valuable in connection with that specific problem. On the procedural questions raised by war in general and the rights of Japanese-Americans in the Second World War in particular, see Nanette Dembitz, "Racial Discrimination and Military Judgment," 45 *Columbia Law Review* 175 (1945) and Charles Fairman, "The Supreme Court on Military Jurisdiction," 59 *Harvard Law Review* 833 (1946). The best general and short account of the Court's doctrines concerning criminal procedure in the states is John R. Green's "The Bill of Rights, the Fourteenth Amendment, and the Supreme Court," 46 *Michigan Law Review* 869 (1948).

The literature on the question of racial discrimination is voluminous. Robert K. Carr, *Federal Protection of Civil Rights* (1947) is a good account of the history of federal legislation in this field and the constitutional problems it raises. J. D. Hyman, "Segregation and the Fourteenth Amendment," 4 *Vanderbilt Law Review* 555 (1951) is a condensed survey of the course of judicial enforcement of the antidiscrimination clauses before the School Segregation decision. Among other essays that I have found particularly rewarding are: Robert J. Harris, "The Constitution, Education, and Segregation," 29 *Temple Law Quarterly* 409 (1956); John P. Roche, "Education, Segregation, and the Supreme Court—a Political Analysis," 99 *University of Pennsylvania Law Review* 949 (1951); and Arthur E. Sutherland, "The American Judiciary and Racial Segregation," 20 *Modern Law Review* 201 (1957).

On the attitude of the Court toward civil liberties in very recent years, see Robert G. McCloskey, "The Supreme Court Finds a Role," 42 *Virginia Law Review* 735 (1956); "Useful Toil or the Paths of Glory?" 43 *Ibid.* 803 (1957); "Tools, Stumbling Blocks and Stepping Stones," 44 *Ibid.* 1029 (1958). Also Alpheus T. Mason and William M. Beaney, *The Supreme Court in a Free Society* (1959); and Charles H. Pritchett, *The Political Offender and the Warren Court* (1958). "Policy-Making in a Democracy: The Role of the United States Supreme Court," 6 *Journal of Public Law* 2 (1957) is a full-dress treatment of many constitutional problems past and present, including a substantial amount of material and comment on the antijudicial movement of the late 1950's. This movement is amply documented in *Hearings* of a sub-committee of the Senate Commitee on the Judiciary on "Limitation of Appellate Jurisdiction of the United States Supreme Court," 85th Cong., 2d Sess. on S. 2646 (1958).

The modern problem of the Court's role, especially in the civil rights field, is treated in the works by Pritchett and Mason and Beaney cited above and in the *Journal of Public Law*, also just cited. Other works have been mentioned earlier in this bibliography, among them Learned Hand's *The Bill of Rights* and Jackson's *The Supreme Court in the American System of Government.* Hand prescribes for the Court an extremely limited function that is, I believe, at odds with historical realities. Herbert Wechsler, "Toward Neutral Principles of Constitutional Law," 73 *Harvard Law Review* 1 (1959) leans somewhat the other way, but expresses a confidence about the intent of the Constitution that is hardly justified by the historical evidence. The volume edited by Arthur E. Sutherland, *Government under Law* (1956), contains a lot of discussion of this problem, some of it rewarding. But America still awaits a treatment that does full justice to the importance and subtlety and intricacy of this issue.

Index

Index

Calhoun, John C.: proponent of states' rights, 77–78

Campbell, John A., 119–20, 128, 139

Cardozo, Justice Benjamin N., 158; dissent favoring minimum wages, 167; fundamental rights protected by Fourteenth Amendment, 205

Catron, Justice John, 95

Charles River Bridge v. *Warren Bridge Co.*, 88

Chase, Chief Justice Salmon P., 93, 102, 113

Chase, Justice Samuel, 37; political partisanship, 38; impeachment, 45–48

Child Labor Tax Case, 142, 145, 184

Chisholm v. *Georgia*, 35, 37, 52

Choate, Joseph H.: "onward march of communism," 124; counsel in income tax case, 140–41, 162

Cincinnati, New Orleans & Texas Pacific Railway Co. v. *I.C.C.*, 126

Civil rights, 170; as dominant judicial question, 181, 192; procedural safeguards, 200–204, 226

Civil Rights Acts, 120

Civil Rights Cases, 210

Cohens v. *Virginia*, 64, 77, 218, 227

Coke, Sir Edward, 11

Commerce Clause, 5, 16; includes navigation, 69; state power to regulate commerce, 87; federal pre-emption and laissez faire, 124, 144; permissive interpretation, 184, 185

Communism, 198–99

Constitution: alterability of meaning, 15; ambiguity, 6; apportionment of direct taxes, 140; bills of credit, 98; clear and present danger, 172, 178; criminal procedures, 170–73, 204–7; commerce, *see* Commerce Clause; contracts, *see* Contract Clause; due process, *see* Due Process; duty on state exports, 43; equal protection, *see* Equal Protection; ex post facto, 16, 50; freedom of expression, speech, 170–72, 196–97, 230; freedom of religion, 197–98; general welfare, 184; grand jury indictment, 173; habeas corpus, 98; impeachment, 45; income tax, 141–42; necessary and proper, 67, 113, 122; preamble, 62; privileges and immunities, 117, 122; procedural rights, 170, 173, 205; ratification, 3; republican form of government, 21; search and seizure, 201–2; self-incrimination, 202; sovereignty, people as source, 62; state action, 208, 212; supremacy clause, 6, 67; titles of nobility, 16; treaty power, 189; *see also* Judiciary

Contract Clause, 6; applicable to contracts of the state, 50–52; strengthened in *Dartmouth College*, 73–75; bankruptcy acts, 78; under the Taney court, 84, 88–89

Cooley v. *Board of Wardens*, 88; later use of pre-emption doctrine, 124, 125, 126, 187; use to forbid segregation, 211

Cooley, Thomas M.: treatise, 131, 162

Corporations: right to sue in federal courts, 84; right to do business in other states, 90; considered "persons," 132

Corwin, Edward S.: critic of court, 163

Court-packing plan: proposed, 169; failure, 175–77

Dartmouth College v. *Woodward*, 73–75, 78

Davis, Justice David, 109, 137

Dayton–Goose Creek Railway, 148

Declaration of Independence: sovereignty from the consent of the governed, 12

Delegation of legislative authority, 166, 188

Dennis v. *United States*, 196–97, 198

Index

Index

Index

53–56; absolute formulation, flexible use, 137–38, 158–65; in subversion cases, 200, 221

Judiciary, 6–7; salaries of judges, 16; tenure during good behavior, 30, 169; controversies between a state and a citizen of another state, 34; appellate power over state courts, 63

Judiciary Act of 1789: passage, 3; content, 4; Section 25, appellate jurisdiction over state courts, 7, 64; Section 13 held invalid, 41; power to review tested, 60–63; Supreme Court emerges as dominant tribunal, 65

Judiciary Act of 1801: enacted, 38; repealed, 39, 47

Labor: yellow dog contracts, 156; picketing and registration of union organizers, 194

Legal fraternity, 72; as court's constituency, 75

Legal realists: court as policymaker, 20, 163; effect on Supreme Court's role, 183

Legal Tender Cases, 115; see also *Hepburn* v. *Griswold*

Lincoln, Abraham: suspension of habeas corpus, 98–99; military trial of civilians, 106–7

Livingston, Robert R., 69

Lochner v. *New York*: limitation of working hours, 153, 156, 157, 159, 162, 178, 186, 194

Louisiana Purchase, 49, 93

Loyalty oaths, 203–4

Madison, James: on judicial supremacy, 9, 11; national bank, 32; states not suable in federal courts, 34, 38, 41; "Mr. Madison's war," 55

Mann Act, 145

Marbury v. *Madison*, 40–44, 45, 47, 137, 227

Marshall, Chief Justice John: nature of judicial power, 2; assumption of policy functions, 16; effect of his personal predilections on Supreme Court powers, 25, 28, 30; states not subject to suit in federal courts, 34, 35; appointment by Adams, 39; establishment of judicial review, 40–44; impeachment threats, 45–47; Burr's trial, 48; state law held unconstitutional, 50; contract clause and natural law, 51, 54, 56; favoring property rights and nationalism, 57; judicial strategy, 58; self-disqualified in *Martin* v. *Hunter's Lessee*, 61, 63, 65; in *McCulloch*, 66; commerce clause, 69; rule of law, 72; contract clause strengthened, *Dartmouth College*, 74; bankruptcy acts, 76; achievements, 77–79; death, 81; contrast with Taney court, 82; venerated, 83; doctrine compared with Taney, 87–90, 137; power to tax involves the power to destroy, 141, 169, 181, 184, 192, 216, 218, 222, 225

Martin v. *Hunter's Lessee*, 60–64, 65

Mayor of New York v. *Miln*, 86

McCardle, Ex parte, 111

McCarthyist spirit, 227

McCray v. *United States*, 142–43

McCulloch v. *Maryland*, 66, 78; applied to salaries of federal employees, 90, 141

McLean, Justice John: nationalist, 88; approval of state bank notes, 89; abolitionist, 94

McReynolds, Justice James C., 215

Merryman, Ex parte, 98–99

Military trials, 106, 111

Miller, Justice Samuel F., 119–20, 122

Milligan, Ex parte, 108–10, 112, 114, 137, 201

Missouri v. *Canada*, 179, 210–11, 215

Minimum hours, 153

Index

Index

Index

Vallandigham, Ex parte, 107, 113
VanDevanter, Justice Willis, 183
Vinson, Chief Justice Fred M., 197
Voting, 212–13

Wabash, St. Louis & Pacific Ry. v.
  Illinois, 125, 126
Waite, Chief Justice Morrison R.,
  124, 125, 129, 130; criteria for rate
  regulation, 156, 218
"War Amendments," 120, 209
War of 1812, 48, 55
Warren, Charles, 125
Warren, Chief Justice Earl, 216

Washington, George, 3, 4; request
  for advisory opinions, 32, 38
Wayne, Justice James M., 109
Webster, Daniel, 73; on the "old
  court," 82
Wiemann v. *Updegraff,* 204
Wilson, Justice James, 35, 39
Wiretapping evidence inadmissible,
  202
Wright, B. F., 132, 151

Yates, Robert, 9
Yazoo land-grant scandal, 49
Yellow dog contracts, 156